MW00325081

Ten Secrets to Success After Graduation

Ten Secrets to Success After Graduation

A collection of inspirational career stories from industry professionals

Nick Wagner Sr.

River
Bend
BOOKSHOP

CONTENTS

Copyright © 2021 by Nick Wagner Sr.

All rights reserved. No part of this book may be reproduced in any manner whatsoever without written permission except in the case of brief quotations embodied in critical articles and reviews.

First Printing, 2021

Dedicated to all of the
amazing mentors who
inspire early career professionals.

Introduction

"Why are you writing a book? You don't even read books." That's what my wife said when I told her I wanted to write this book. I laughed a little and told her that this was a way for me to give back, inspire others and share valuable advice from some of the most amazing people I know. I could tell she had concerns: How much time would this take? Who would contribute? Who would edit it? She has known me for more than fifteen years and has learned that when I want something, the activator and achiever in me will make it happen.

That conversation happened during the summer of 2019. It took time and *a lot* of editing, but with the help of some amazing, inspirational people, I got it done.

I wrote a book.

I did not grow up thinking I would ever write a book. According to the CliftonStrengths assessment, communication is one of my top five strengths, but the written word has never been my preferred method of communicating. I can talk to anyone, love telling stories and create and deliver presentations with ease, but writing has never been my thing. I knew I couldn't do this alone, and that is why I asked for help from my friends.

As you read this book, I hope you enjoy the stories from our contributors who have bravely shared some of their most personal moments of success, failure and perseverance. Some of the stories will make you wonder, some will make you cry, some will make you laugh, but I hope all will inspire and empower you.

Our stories are from a diverse group of contributors. You will hear from baby boomers, Gen X and Millennials. Some of our contributors are still working today, while others have retired from their full-time careers and moved on to something different. They work in a variety of industries, including information technology, entertainment and human resources. Some are entrepreneurs, and some work in corporate America. While all are very different, I picked these people specifically due to their unique perspectives on life.

I urge you to keep an open mind as you read each chapter. Not every story will resonate with you, not every story will be relevant to you, and not every story will make you want to change the world. Everyone is different. What drives us is different, and what inspires us is different. I do, however, believe that you will learn something that you didn't know before opening, downloading or listening to this book.

Each chapter begins with the bios of the individuals sharing their stories and how you can connect with them. At the end of each chapter, I share actions for you to take. This could be an activity or assessment to complete or advice on how to take the next step.

While you are reading, feel free to take notes, underline words that resonate with you and think about how you can apply this to your life. The chapters do not need to be read in order, and you do not have to read the book all at one time. You choose how to consume the content. I hope you enjoy the book, and I thank you for giving me the opportunity to empower and inspire you.

Nick Wagner Sr.

Real Life is Hard

You will hear from Nick Wagner Sr.

Bio for Nick:

Nick Wagner Sr. is a husband, father and son. His passion for people is what drives him in his corporate work at Cigna as a human resources professional and with the nonprofit, CITE Inc. he launched with his wife. As a lifelong entrepreneur, Nick is always starting new initiatives and trying to give back to the community and inspire individuals. He hopes this book will do just that—inspire people to reach their Full Potential. The Full Potential Movement is an initiative Nick created under his non-profit to assist people with their careers. This is the first book in what Nick is calling the Full Potential book series.

Connect with Nick:

Email: nickwagner@outlook.com
LinkedIn: linkedin.com/in/nickwagnersr
Website: www.nickwagnersr.com
Website: www.FullPotentialMovement.com

Real Life

When I decided to write this book, I immediately knew what I wanted to focus on in Chapter 1. For years, I've talked to mentees, early career associates and coworkers about how hard real life is on a day-to-day basis. I define real life as your experiences post-school, whether it be high school, community college or a four-year university. You finish school and before you know it:

You find a job or start a business.
You get your own place.
You have bills.
You have responsibilities.
You may be diagnosed with an illness.
You fall in love.
You have a bad breakup.
You get married.
You buy a house.
You have children.
You need to save for retirement.
You start taking care of your parents.
You lose a parent.
Etc.

All of these things are hard. NONE of them are easy. But think about this: When you are in school, you get a teacher, a syllabus, and peers to help you along the journey. Sure, school is challenging, but it is structured, and there are many resources in place to help you succeed. Real life post-school is VERY different.

There is no syllabus for life. There is no teacher. For most young people, real life is about making mistakes and surviving (and learning from) their consequences. If you are successful at overcoming these obstacles, this can be an exciting and powerful experience. But for many of us, it can be difficult and lead us to make poor life decisions. You quickly realize how tough life can be when you don't have step-by-step instructions for the next three months. Once school is over, the structure you have been so accustomed to since you were a kid disappears. This is the first time being on your own. Whom do you turn to for advice? How do you know whom to trust?

Decision-making is an important skill no matter your age. As a preschooler: *Do I eat the Play-Doh?* In elementary school: *What should I get for dessert at lunch?* In middle school: *Should I ask this boy or girl to the school dance?* In high school: *Am I going to college or getting a job?* As you grow, your decisions carry more weight, especially post-school:

Is this apartment the right one?
Which company do I go with for car insurance?
Do I stay at my current job or take a different opportunity?
How much money should I save each month for an emergency fund?
Should I pick the HRA or HSA health plan?
Am I too young to get married?

To answer these questions and countless others, I recommend building a team of people you can trust. This Support System is your group of go-to people for this journey called life. This team could include family, friends, coworkers, mentors, etc. No matter who they are, you should be able to trust them and get real, timely, informative advice from them. Now you may be asking yourself, *Do I need to formally ask someone to be part of my Support System? Is there an application process?* In Chapter 2, I will explore in detail how to build your Support System and why having this group of people is critical to your success.

So, how did I figure all of this out, and what makes me qualified to give you this advice? I'm sure some of you will ask that as you read this book. I will be the first to admit that I have not figured it all out.

I learn something new every day. I have also experienced many successes and made many mistakes. Through each of those experiences, I learned something. And every time I learned something, I wanted to share my learnings.

Leveraging what you have learned from your experiences and from others is what you need to be successful in life. You meet individuals every day who are thriving, and you meet individuals every day who are struggling. What sets them apart? Why do some thrive and some struggle? I believe it is a combination of knowledge, determination and taking the right opportunities.

* * *

Activity: Moments

I hope that this first chapter has shown you that there are many things in life that can go well and that can go wrong. It is how you react to each event that determines your path forward.

At the end of each chapter, I will assign you an activity to help you apply what you have learned. Your homework for this chapter is to document defining moments in your life post-school. These can be positive moments that you want to celebrate as well as moments of opportunity that could have gone better.

We often dwell on the moments of opportunity without celebrating those positive moments. The intent of this exercise is to help you identify all the positive things going on in your life and realize you are doing many things very well.

Positive Moments

_____
_____
_____
_____
_____
_____
_____
_____
_____
_____

Moments of Opportunity

_____
_____
_____
_____
_____
_____
_____
_____
_____
_____

2

Your Support System

You will hear from Nick Wagner Sr. and Gary Burnham Jr.

Bio for Nick:

Nick Wagner Sr. is a husband, father and son. His passion for people is what drives him in his corporate work at Cigna as a human resources professional and with the nonprofit, CITE Inc. he launched with his wife. As a lifelong entrepreneur, Nick is always starting new initiatives and trying to give back to the community and inspire individuals. He hopes this book will do just that—inspire people to reach their Full Potential. The Full Potential Movement is an initiative Nick created under his non-profit to assist people with their careers. This is the first book in what Nick is calling the Full Potential book series.

Connect with Nick:

Email: nickwagner@outlook.com
LinkedIn: linkedin.com/in/nickwagnersr
Website: www.nickwagnersr.com
Website: www.FullPotentialMovement.com

Surround Yourself With Amazing People

When you need to make an important decision, either personally or professionally, whom do you call? How do you make your decision? Some of us like to write down the pros and cons of the decision. Some of us call our parents or our friends. Some of us may even flip a coin.

I have probably done all of the above, but after years of trial and error, I believe I figured this out. Now, when I need to make an important decision, I leverage my Support System that I have been putting together over the past two decades.

My Support System consists of family members, friends, colleagues, mentors and professionals. These are the individuals I meet with, call and text when I need advice on a difficult decision.

Let me walk you through some examples of how I have used my Support System and why their advice helped me find the clarity I needed.

Situation 1: Small Business Financial Crisis

It was the summer of 2007, and the sun was shining. It was warm, but not too hot. I was in a great mood because I had tickets to see a Boston Red Sox game at Fenway Park in Boston that evening. At the time, I was working at my business, North American Motorsports, an e-commerce startup selling aftermarket car parts for European cars. We purchased our inventory using business credit cards to help manage our cash flow and rack up those fantastic credit card rewards points.

That day we received a letter from our credit card company, and it stated that as part of their standard process, they reviewed our account and were implementing a limit on our credit card purchases.

I immediately had that pit in my stomach that you get when something doesn't feel right. How were we going to pay for our inventory? We were growing every month, which meant we had to buy more inventory, but how would we do this? We called a meeting of the four owners to discuss options.

The four of us quickly realized that while we had some potential answers to solve this issue, we needed help. I remember suggesting we call two people to assist us in determining possible solutions: my father, who had a degree in finance from MIT, and our accountant.

I gave away the tickets to the baseball game that night and set up a meeting for later that evening. This was too important to wait until the next day, and both my father and our accountant agreed they could meet. The four of us were beyond stressed about what we thought was a massive financial issue for our company. My father arrived first and helped calm us down, do a quick review of our financials and prepare questions for the accountant. We explained the situation to the accountant when he arrived, and within ten minutes, the problem was solved. TEN MINUTES. Our accountant advised us to ask our suppliers for term payments, where we would have a certain number of days to pay them via check instead of using a credit card. He informed us that this was a standard process to purchase inventory across many industries, and he assumed many of our vendors would have no issue doing this for us.

He was right. The next day we worked with a handful of vendors, set up payment terms with them and stopped paying for our inventory from them with a credit card. The financial crisis was solved because I leveraged my Support System to get advice from people who had seen this situation before.

Situation 2: New Job Opportunity with a Growing Family

In the spring of 2013, my wife was pregnant with our second child, and my son, who had been born in early 2012, was keeping us very busy. Life at home was beautiful, exciting and chaotic. I was working in information technology for Eric Consolazio (a contributor in Chapter 7 of this book), who was one of the most inspirational leaders I had ever met. I was his chief of staff but was looking for my next opportunity to get back into project management.

Eric had finalized an agreement with a large technology company in South Korea and was looking for someone to manage the project. He knew I was seeking a new opportunity and asked me if I would be interested. I was humbled, excited and terrified all at the same time.

Questions started running through my head as Eric was sharing more details. What is the time difference between the East Coast of the U.S. and South Korea? How long is the flight to get there? Would the project be over before November, when my wife was due with our second child?

I obtained as much information as I could from the conversation, thanked Eric for offering me the opportunity and let him know that I would have to discuss it with my wife.

I called my wife and one of my best friends immediately after the meeting to discuss the opportunity. I told them both that I thought the position would be interesting, challenging and great for my career. But I also felt that I would not be able to make it work. How was I going to work on a project with a team that was 14 hours ahead (due to the time difference) with a young family at home? What would my wife think if I had to travel to South Korea multiple times in the next year during the end of her pregnancy and immediately following the birth of our child?

Through multiple conversations with my wife and my friend, I concluded that if I took this job, I would fail at home and at work by not being able to meet the expectations of either. They both helped me document how to tell my manager that I was not interested so I could clearly articulate my reasoning. Looking back, this was absolutely the right decision for my family and the right decision for my career. My Support System enabled me to feel confident with the decision of saying no to the opportunity, and I am thankful every day to have both of these amazing people in my life.

I have shared two difficult situations in my career where I used my Support System to help make decisions and solve problems. Your Support System is not only available for major career decisions or crises. They are also there to motivate you, inspire you, listen to you vent or even just talk. This group of individuals is critical to your success in the journey of life. Listening to the opinions, thoughts and experiences of others will help you make more informed decisions. The activity at the end of this chapter will help you identify your own Support System. This next story will give you a few more examples of how they can be there to help you.

* * *

Bio for Gary:

Gary Burnham Jr. is a retired Hall of Fame professional baseball player who played eleven years in Major League Baseball organizations (as part of the Phillies, Blue Jays, Reds and Cardinals) and on three international teams (Taiwan, Japan and Italy). Gary was an All-American baseball player at Clemson University (1994-1997) and an All-American baseball player at South Windsor High School in Connecticut (1993). He battled through more than ten orthopedic operations on his knees and shoulders during his baseball career.

Gary is a sales professional and landlord as well as a part-time baseball instructor. He and his wife, Rachel, have three amazing children.

Connect with Gary:

Email: garyburnhamjr@gmail.com
LinkedIn: linkedin.com/in/garyrburnhamjr

People I Call On in a Dark Place

When I think back on times I've struggled, faced adversity or found my-self in do-or-die, back-against-the-wall situations, there were always a few go-to people in my life whom I turned to for support and advice.

I always saw these people as pillars of strength who could understand my feelings and encourage me to forge ahead and use my struggles to strengthen my determination to achieve my goals. Throughout my life and career, several people have filled this role for me—each one is part of my Support System.

From the time I was a teenager, my uncle Ralph was one of these people for me. Only twelve years older than me, he had played professional baseball like I wanted to and had a successful sales career. I grew up fol-lowing in his footsteps and idolized him as a mentor and role model. To me, he was a real-life example of mental toughness and grit, a guy con-stantly preaching, "Work out until you puke," "Hit until your hands bleed," or "Run a million sprints or more." I always knew a call with him would leave me filled with positive energy by the time I got off the phone. I remember a time I was struggling with my hitting in 2001—I was feeling frustrated and down, and I didn't know how I was going to overcome the challenge I was facing. When I called Uncle Ralph, I vividly remember him believing in me more than I believed in myself. He reassured me that I was a great hitter and that the answer was to out-work everyone else and to have the courage to face adversity head-on, look it in the eye and overcome it. It was always comforting to hear that I was not alone, that how I felt was more common than I thought, and that there were ways to solve the problems I was facing. As I grew up, my relationship with Uncle Ralph was incredibly important to me developing strong character and fortitude.

I have also relied a lot on my mom for support and strength throughout my life. Several times during my baseball career, I remember calling home and telling her I simply forgot how to hit. My mother's response was usually, and comfortingly, predictable: "Swing the bat!" "You're the best!" "You were born and bred to be a baseball player!" This was all I needed to hear, and I usually hung up the phone with steam coming out of my ears, ready and motivated to play my best and confident I could.

Two other people in my Support System were my Clemson University baseball coaches, Jack Leggett and Tim Corbin. They were both living examples of hard work, dedication, commitment and character. I always looked up to these men tremendously; both were tireless workers—personally and professionally—and I really admired that about them.

Jack and Tim would constantly preach "Pain, torture, agony" as we did our physical conditioning in the South Carolina August heat before fall ball started to build our mental toughness to an incredible level. There is one time I remember like it was yesterday—we used to get tested in a 2.3-mile run as a team, and both Jack and Tim finished in the top ten out of thirty players. What made it so impressive was that they were 40 years old at the time, and my teammates and I were 20. Later in life, during personal times of struggle, I would revisit this training in my mind, and I could hear the coaches in my ear, motivating me to keep going. It helped me to know that there was always one more lap or one more rep left in me. I modeled my behavior after what they taught me, and when the going got tough, I felt I often had the advantage over others because I had undergone this training that enabled me to remain mentally tough in all situations. Having these two people in my life helped me become a stronger, more successful person.

When I reached the highest levels of professional sports—levels never experienced by my friends, family or coaches—it was more important for me to be self-reliant. Through intense physical training sessions, mainly completed alone, I developed a hardened mind that simply never stopped forging ahead regardless of adversity or stress. During long road trips, I spent many nights alone in my hotel room, knocking out several hundred push-ups and sit-ups, and I would run on the hotel treadmill long into the early morning hours, watching SportsCenter on ESPN to keep me company. I believe I was prepared for this time in my life in part because of the lessons I had learned from my Support System.

Right about the time I felt I had mastered these internal strength skills, my wife entered my life. From the moment we met, she has reinforced the importance of these skills through her actions. She is incredibly self-disciplined, as she has a background in gymnastics, and she is familiar with the benefits of follow-through and perseverance. I love how she supports and encourages me and is quick to remind me that the discipline I learned playing sports is the same one needed for my family and career. I am forever grateful she is in my life, and she is a big reason why I am where I am today.

All in all, my courage to forge ahead is one of the foundational skills that has allowed me to achieve the success that I have achieved. The foundation of this fortitude and tenacity was first built by my uncle and my mom, who were in my ear all the time when I needed it the most, and is now reinforced by my wife.

To have these people in my life willing to listen and offer support and advice is a blessing. It had a profound effect on building my character, and it still does. I would encourage everyone to find that person or people in their life whom they can lean on during challenging times for positive words and strength, and to harness the power of those words to call upon them when in need.

Activity: Identify Your Support System

Many of us have a Support System but have never taken the time to document who these individuals are and assess if we need any additional people.

Your needs for a Support System will vary based on your personal life and professional career. Do not compare your Support System with someone else's; everyone's will be different. Please use this activity as a guide to understand the type of resources that could be in your Support System. Next, identify people to add to your Support System and document how they may be able to help.

Potential People for Your Support System

Family Member

- How do they help you personally and professionally?
- What do you typically discuss with them?
- What can they say to you that no one else can?

Friend

- How can they help you view situations differently?
- Since they are not a family member, can they help you with personal situations?
- Are they able to provide you with unbiased guidance about work that a colleague may not be able to?

Colleague

- Since they understand your company culture, they can typically help with work-related questions.
- Try to find someone you can trust that you can ask for career advice.

Manager

- No one cares about your career as much as you, but finding a manager who truly invests in your career will help you be more successful at work.
- A good manager will be able to tell you what you do well and identify your opportunities for improvement.

Other Possible People:

Mentor
Sponsor
Coach
Therapist
Support Group
Professor/Teacher
Faith-Based Professional (e.g., Priest, Rabbi, etc.)

Identify and Document Your Support System

Name: _____

How they can help:

_____

_____

_____

Name: _____

How they can help:

_____

_____

_____

Name: _____

How they can help:

_____

_____

_____

Name: _____

How they can help:

_____

_____

_____

Name: _____

How they can help:

_____

_____

_____

Name: _____

How they can help:

_____

_____

_____

Name: _____

How they can help:

_____

_____

_____

Name: _____

How they can help:

_____

_____

_____

Name: _____

How they can help:

_____

_____

_____

3

The Importance of Family and Friends

You will hear from Matt Williams and Eric Sherman.

Bio for Matt:

Matt Williams graduated from Syracuse University in 2003 and is currently serving as Supervising Producer for Nat Geo Wild's "Secrets of the Zoo" franchise. Over the last eighteen years, Matt has directed, produced and written hundreds of hours of content for various networks including CMT, MTV, VH1, A&E, USA, HGTV, El Rey, and Nat Geo Wild. Matt currently lives just outside of Tampa, Florida, with his wife, Alycia, and daughter, Emilia.

Connect with Matt:

Email: mjwilliams81@aol.com
LinkedIn: linkedin.com/in/matthewjameswilliams/

Hallmark Christmas Movie Epiphany

Ever hate-watch a Hallmark movie? My wife and I do all the time. They are the worst...yet simultaneously the best movies ever. You know what you are getting with a Hallmark movie—usually it's about a small-town girl who runs into a workaholic guy who initially comes off abrasive, but the two are thrust together to unexpectedly work together on some sort of holiday pageant. One thing leads to another, and they fall in love. Almost every time, this happens when the main character prioritizes love and family over work. There is a reason Hallmark uses this formula seemingly every single time—they understand who their audience is, and the idea of prioritizing love over work resonates with a lot of people out there.

I can relate. I am a freelance TV producer, and I love what I do. I have seen forty-nine states and a dozen countries on somebody else's dime. I traveled more in my twenties alone than most people get to in their entire life. I get to be creative and work with fun people in a super relaxed environment. I do not own a tie. So, there's a lot to like! Conversely, it is not all rainbows and Instagram filters; it is a grueling profession. I probably averaged six months on the road for most of my twenties. That was a lot of uncomfortable plane rides, subpar hotel beds, and living out of suitcases. Basically, as a freelancer, I work gig to gig. Sometimes I will work for a year straight without any real time off; other times I have gone several months in between jobs. People in my industry tend to keep taking work because you never know when the proverbial work well will dry up, only to find yourself unemployed, sitting in your underwear, watching SportsCenter reruns until the TV turns itself off due to inactivity. (That was pretty much my entire winter in 2009.)

Like many people in my industry and others, I spent the majority of my twenties focused on career advancement. Fresh out of college with tons of energy, I thought that this was just what you did. I treated it like the NCAA March Madness Tournament: Survive and advance! And it worked—I was directing shows and being well-compensated for it by the age of 27. But in doing so, there were sacrifices that had to be made along the way. I missed out on friends' weddings, family reunions, birthday parties, vacations with friends, even a few funerals. So, was it worth it? It's complicated.

Let me be clear: I do not regret how I lived my twenties, in large part because advancing my career in my twenties has now given me more freedom to turn down work. I definitely feel like I have re-prioritized my life, now that I'm deep into my thirties. I met my wife, Alycia, about eight years ago, and she has definitely contributed to my shift in life priorities. She is also a producer, yet she will miss out on shows and months of work if it interferes with her yearly trip to Greece to visit family. If she loses work because of it, she is unfazed. I admire the hell out of that, and it really got my wheels turning—is another promotion worth missing out on more life events? Is $200 or $500 more a week worth never being able to go on a vacation again? Do I need the extra anxiety of always being attached to my phone, checking emails 24/7? Is vying for an "executive producer" title really going to fulfill my life any more than it already is? For me, the answer is a resounding no, and that is a word I have had to start using a lot more often. It is not easy turning down work and missing out on dream shows I would have loved to work on, but for me, it is still better than missing out on life.

In 2020, my wife and I welcomed Emmie, our first child, into the world, and putting an emphasis on family time over work has never been clearer. Being a good father and husband is now at the top of my priority list. As for work, I still may have to travel a little bit, but I am going to do everything in my power to be home with my family and be there to see every one of my daughter's milestones. Work is just a paycheck at this point, a means to provide my family with the best, most comfortable life I can possibly provide. Any additional career aspirations I may have once had have vanished, and I don't have any regrets.

Everyone is different, and I'm not sure anyone can tell you how to prioritize your life. But I do feel confident that at some point in your life, whether it is fresh out of college or late into your thirties, you'll have your own Hallmark Christmas movie epiphany.

* * *

Bio for Eric:

Eric Sherman has spent twenty years in the hospitality industry. Over the course of that time, he graduated from serving tables to serving as the manager of several establishments. During the first ten years of his career, he routinely worked at multiple restaurants simultaneously, resulting in a hectic life with little free time.

In 2020, Eric renewed his pursuit of a bachelor's degree at Oregon State University. Prior to this, he had been absent from higher education for a decade after attending four schools in nine years and not finding a good fit. He has also been taking classes to earn certifications in several computer programming languages to help him transition out of the hospitality industry and into a new career.

Connect with Eric:

Email: ericvsherman@gmail.com
LinkedIn: linkedin.com/in/eric-v-sherman/

Life is Short

"Time has a wonderful way to show us what really matters." –Margaret Peters

I was cruising the internet when I stumbled upon a LinkedIn post from an old friend—he announced that he was putting together this very book. I knew immediately that I wanted to contribute so that I could share the lessons that we are discussing right now: the value of time with family and friends. I hope that my words will help many others, but even if only one person takes something away from this section, it will be completely worth it.

To begin, I first must mention that I do not regret my choices in life, as they made me who I am. I dropped out of college about a half dozen times, but that was necessary for me to find out who I needed to be. It led me to the path of hospitality, where I flourished. You do not sustain a career arc for twenty years without some level of success, even if that success is just survival. The hospitality industry is tough because people can be tough, and working in it forges you as if you were a hammer in an old blacksmith's shop. You become more patient and kinder to strangers, and you also become more aware of how people treat each other. It becomes easier to spot those who have spent time doing this type of work for a living from those who have not, and I have learned valuable lessons about every facet of business and personal interactions. The industry brought me great highs, but I have also hit a few fairly unenviable lows during my time as well.

The hospitality industry is tough not only because you often have to manage difficult people and difficult situations, but you also have to work when most people aren't. For the industry itself to thrive, the inherent schedule is nights and weekends. That means you often miss birthdays, weddings, gatherings, babies being born, and scores of events with your friends and family. The longer I worked in the industry and maintained the "typical" schedule, the more I realized that I would not have unlimited time to see my parents, both of whom I was seeing about two to three times per year. I realized that I would not have unlimited time to see my friends, whom I saw three to four times in a decade. These became unbearable statistics of the life I had chosen, and once I identified that time with family and friends was a priority for me, I knew I needed to make a change.

And that is why we are here, gathered around the fire, listening to the elder hospitality worker talk. I metaphorically chose to walk uphill in the snow both ways through life, and perhaps I can give somebody here a sled for at least the ride home.

What do I mean by that last sentence? Well, the hardest thing for me has been transitioning out of the industry, and I want others to learn from my experience. If you read my bio, you will see that my college experience was more akin to a drive-thru meal than a sit-down dinner. I tried it; it was sloppy, half-cooked and mostly wrong; and I drove away too fast and left my cookie at the window. This means that as I approach 40 years old, I'm figuring out how to live my life, support my entrepreneur girlfriend and pay our mortgage, all while cooking up a career exit strategy.

So, what would I have done differently? If I could hop in a time machine and tell my younger self just one piece of information, what would it be? I have an easy answer to that, and it could possibly be the easiest conversation I have had in a long time. I would sit myself down and explain that I need to stick it out in school, if only to earn that piece of paper. I would remind myself that I can still party and work the hospitality life, but at some point (and I would be speaking from experience to myself), I am going to want more time with family and friends than that schedule allows, and a degree will give me more options to make that happen. I will need to have the exit plan ready so I can pull the parachute and jump out of the plane the instant that I want to.

If you find yourself in a situation like mine, figure out what makes you happy and prioritize that. For me, as an old guy leaving the hospitality industry in the rearview mirror, it is time with my loved ones. Everything I do now directly reflects the goal I have to see them more, because time with friends and family is paramount to me.

What can you take from this? My message is simple: Find out what is important to you and make time for it. Set up monthly family dinners. Schedule time to meet up with friends. If your career has you on an "alternate" schedule, it will be up to you to find a way to get a weekend night off. Make it work, because you will not get that time back. And if all that fails, find a new career, like I am. It is only too late if you let it be.

Activity: Create a Family and Friends Bucket List

One thing I want to do this week:

_____

_____

_____

Two things I want to do this month:

_____

_____

_____

_____

_____

_____

Five things I want to do this year:

_____

_____

_____

_____

_____

_____

_____

_____

4

Focus on Building Relationships

You will hear from John M. Jaramillo and David Salinas.

Bio for John:

John M. Jaramillo's diverse background of education in marketing, organizational psychology, mediation and business administration; his work in various industries; the relationships and connections he's made; and his family, including his wife and two sons, have all contributed to who he is and what he delivers to both his own relationships and clients through his business Coach It Out, LLC.

Connect with John:

Email: johnmjaramillo@coachitout.com
Website: coachitout.com
LinkedIn: linkedin.com/in/jmjaramillo/

Success is Everywhere

No matter what your definition of success is, it's there, all around you, for the taking. And from what I have seen in my coaching practice, Coach It Out LLC., the main and most destructive obstacle to that success is easy to spot.

It's us.

Whether we know it or not, most of us are doing ourselves in. We limit our own achievements and forward progress by contributing to our own obstacles and pitfalls—the same obstacles and pitfalls we lament and complain about.

But please don't take my word for it. If you think about your own life and experiences, especially times when things didn't work out, you'll probably find there were moments where you had more control than you believed at the time—and you know and can see it now. One of those areas in which we have control is building relationships. We need to consider what we are really putting into—and getting out of—the connections around us.

Relationships can take so many forms. Nowadays, the growing concern about relationships is whether they're a matter of substance versus appearance, depth versus façade. Just take a look at social media and where so many people get trapped: the value they assign to the number of likes, connections, and comments their posts draw and the appearance of the seemingly idyllic lives and careers of others.

To avoid falling victim to that pressure of appearance in your life and work, as you make your way down those paths, make sure to really connect with the people around you. I know, I know -- it sounds so simple, right? It sounds like obvious, common sense. Unfortunately, though, it's not common practice.

The connection I'm talking about—where we truly understand each other—is not just meeting and knowing people but also diving behind the façade and appearance, deeper into who people are, what they're capable of, and what they desire for themselves.

In that process, you're proactively looking for, seeing, and contributing to the value in others, both the value they already share and the value you can help them discover in themselves.

Unfortunately, people instead tend to be much too reactive in relationships, barely taking the time or making the commitment to get the best out of both themselves and others through that mutual connection.

And listen, truth be told, I don't have a particular story for building relationships. One story just wouldn't be enough. Any relationship story I pick to share here would be too unique to its own web of players, circumstances, and lessons to apply to those reading this.

In my life and career, I've seen what people can leave on the table when they don't harness their relationships effectively. As a kid, I was shy, unconfident, and an introvert – the holy triad of quiet. With this quiet triad -- or Qui-ad (?) -- of attributes came an evolving power of observation of the world around me.

I wasn't so quiet that I had trouble making friends, but I was quiet enough that my observation-to-participation ratio was easily 3-to-1. As a result, I eventually grew to be fascinated watching people, asking questions, and taking in everything around me.

I still am.

And even though that Quiad (yes, I just coined a word) still exists in me, it's subtle, and, even better, I have harnessed it for my career and personal and professional development.

I am still very much the observer wherever I go. I still see what others do not or sometimes cannot: We do not tap into our relationships in the right way.

And my observations don't mean that I know what relationships should look like. Just like anything we want to develop, there is no cookie-cutter path for how to build relationships. Building relationships is different from one pairing of people to the next. It's all about how deep we personally need and want to go and what kind of substance we want to create.

Leadership coaching includes proactively analyzing relationships and learning what someone's expectations are of others. Each of us has our own view of what a relationship should be. But what is *your* standard for relationships? Is it working for or against you?

You can set yourself apart from others based on how you respect your relationships. So, when it comes to building relationships, please...

...Be Who You Are

Being—and constantly improving upon—who you really are will serve you best in the end. Being someone you're not for the sake of meeting and impressing others will only do you in. Building a façade may be easy, but you'll burn out later when the need to keep up appearances catches up with you. There is strength in your genuineness. Through that strength you can provide your best to other people.

...Know What You Can Provide Others

This is my shortest piece of advice because it covers a topic I know nothing about: you. You as an individual have a message to share and a story to tell. You dictate the narrative of what others know and see of you. Don't take that for granted. Don't squander it. Don't wait on others to demonstrate what you are all about.

...Do Not Cheapen Your Worth

The hardest part about building relationships for each of us is finding the right people. The spectrum of people available for us to meet reflects different styles, attributes, motivations, skills, desires, etc., and ranges from the greatest of considerate and contributing partners to those who are selfish and merely take from a relationship. Know what the best relationships would look like for you and set that standard.

...Find Your Tribe

We cannot be anything or anybody without others who serve as an audience for our message. They help us. They make us. They can bring out the best in us, sharpening and challenging us to do better. And we should be all those things in return to others. A relationship goes both ways. (Again, common sense, uncommon practice.) Finding great relationships is a numbers game, one of trial and error. Don't merely settle for who you have around you. You become what you tolerate.

...Practice Stellar Customer Service

Aside from knowing what you can provide, carefully execute how you deliver it. Think about the experience you help create for others. Do you know what they need? Do you know what drives and motivates them? How do they feel when they're around you? What do they take away? People put different amounts of effort into their connections, so set yourself apart.

...Never Judge a Book by Its Cover

You often cannot know who someone truly is based on just one quick conversation or meeting in passing. It takes a while for most people to show others who they really are. Never believe you have their value pegged based on one encounter. It takes more time to truly get to know someone and build a possibly great relationship.

Looking for the best in others brings out the best in you, whether you're networking for your business or job, entering a mentoring or coaching relationship, or building a new friendship.

The hardest part about building relationships is that it takes time to find and build the right ones. The trial and error of finding the right people is part of the journey—and well worth it. But most of us want a taste of the end result before taking that journey. That just can't happen.

Demonstrate to people the high standard you have for what can be done for others, a standard in which everyone gets better and everyone can win.

Demonstrate that a connection with you is not about quantity but quality.

* * *

Bio for David:

David Salinas is a serial entrepreneur and investor. In 2007, he co-founded Digital Surgeons and served as its CEO for more than a decade. Under his leadership, the agency delivered award-winning results for clients like Lady Gaga and the U.S Open.

While CEO of Digital Surgeons, David has partnered and launched numerous businesses, including founding and serving as the visionary behind District, a $25 million start-up ecosystem and real estate development in New Haven, Connecticut.

David recognized workforce talent was a key pillar to the local economy and start-up ecosystem, so he founded and chairs District Arts + Education (DAE), a nonprofit with a mission of providing educational and developmental opportunities that prepare individuals for meaningful data and digital-centric careers that serve humanity, build community, and deepen health and prosperity for all.

Connect with David:

LinkedIn: linkedin.com/in/davidsalinas/
Instagram: @igrowbrands
Twitter: @igrowbrands

Who's in Your Contact List?

Early on in my life, I learned two powerful adages that would become part of the foundation for my success:

"Your network is your net worth," and "It's not what you know but who you know."

Those two statements would guide my rise from "a guy who knows no one" to "the guy who knows everyone." It helped me become a successful entrepreneur, build multiple multimillion-dollar companies, and create opportunities for myself and others in unbelievable, unconventional ways.

It allowed my partner and I to start our first business: a creative consultancy called Digital Surgeons with $5,000 and no clients or network. However, in less than four years, we were working with Lady Gaga on a campaign that would win us a Webby Award (the Grammys of the internet).

After nine years with Digital Surgeons, my relationships and networking skills would sit at the nucleus of a strategy that would help us acquire 9.5 acres of land and a roughly 200,000-square-foot abandoned building from the government for just $1. That's right, one dollar. This became District, a $25,000,000-plus real estate development and start-up campus and a leading example of what's new and modern in the state of Connecticut.

All of this started with the initial investment of just $5,000. No angel investors, venture capitalists or debt providers would ever play a big part in these journeys, only relationships and world-class network engineering.

Your Network is Your Net Worth

Growing up poor, a son of an immigrant union worker in New York City, meant my net worth and my network were both starting from zero. Right after college, when I was starting my career, I met an advisor who said, "Your network is your net worth." It resonated with me, and I went on to over index on networking to hone my skills and increase my worth. It was hard at first. Sometimes it felt like I was wasting my time, but in actuality I was honing the craft and becoming a better networker and, eventually, a network engineer.

In the traditional sense, a network engineer is a technologist who maintains IT systems (networks). Below are the qualities you need to be good in this position:

- An analytical mind.
- An ability to learn new technologies quickly.
- Good time management skills.
- An ability to follow processes.
- Strong documentation skills.
- Good communication skills—both written and verbal.

To be the kind of network engineer I'm referring to is a bit different, but they share a lot of similarities. See below how the differences between the two network engineers unfold:

- An analytical mind. -> Visualize and analyze your people networks. Connect dots quickly. Solve problems. Be effective.
- An ability to learn new technologies quickly. -> Learn about new people quickly. You can do this by asking yourself, *Where are they? How do I reach them? Whom do they know? What do they care about? What makes them tick? What are their goals? Are they closed or open networks?*
- Good time management skills. -> This is not just about managing your time; it's about respecting the time of others. Never waste anyone's time. Be precise and conscientious with their calendar and yours.
- An ability to follow processes. -> Rome wasn't built in a day and neither are relationships. Some can take years. Take your time, focus and follow the process. Rushing things can be a huge turnoff. Give more away unconditionally: time, advice, etc. You will get value back when the time is right and you shoot the right shot.
- Strong documentation skills. -> This can be mental documentation or written. It could be as simple as keeping a note about someone's children's names in your phone or remembering a birthday. In my case, I recall settings (places), clothing, business card colors, and unique details about people, situations and scenarios.
- Good communication skills. -> This one is the same, because written and verbal communication skills are important no matter what you're doing.

It's Not What You Know But Who You Know

To this day, my friend Pete and I laugh and say, "If we only knew back then that you go to Yale or Harvard for the network and not the education, we would've done things differently and been better students."

You can be the most popular guy among 19-year-olds, and that will gain you great connections with 19-year-olds. If you want your network to add value to your life, you need to seek out new energy and value in your networking. Spend less time learning about things and more time learning about people.

To do that, I have focused on two things:

1. Whom I speak to.
2. How I show up.

Your network must be diverse. Diversity means differences in age, gender, color, stage of life, wealth, professions, professional positions, and more, and young adults often do not spend enough time talking to wise, older folks. Do not wait for them to engage with you; go out there and start the conversations.

One of my early advisors used to jokingly call himself a "gray hair." And young people often have an aversion to gray hairs, thinking they are out of touch with the world today. But this mentality will hurt your network, because older people have experience, wisdom and deep, well-built networks that they can tap into when they trust you. So, talk to everyone and learn from them, no matter their age.

The opposite is true of older people and networking with younger adults. There is so much to learn and gain from youthful people, and I have learned from their example over the years. Energy, wonder and, in many cases, different wisdom can be found in younger people. So, be just as open to giving to those who seem to have nothing left to learn.

Other forms of diversity are important as well, especially ethnicity and race. In life, you will come across many cultures. Understanding those cultures or at least empathizing with them will help you to make more friends.

In closing, I would say to follow these key tenets.

- Bring the right energy.
- Mean what you say and say what you mean.
- Be memorable.

You are a brand, and brands are built through experiences and relationships with people.

* * *

Activity: Connect 5

Deepen your connection with five people who are currently in your network.

Look for five new relationships that would benefit you personally or professionally. Reach out to each person and set up a meeting either in person or virtually.

Name: _____

Reason for connecting:

_____

_____

_____

Name: _____

Reason for connecting:

_____

_____

_____

Name: _____

Reason for connecting:

_____

_____

_____

Name: _____

Reason for connecting:

_____

_____

_____

Name: _____

Reason for connecting:

_____

_____

_____

5

Don't Be Afraid to Ask for Help

You will hear from Shannon Malkin Daniels and Michelle Puzzo.

Bio for Shannon:

Shannon Malkin Daniels is an entrepreneur, author and professional speaker who views obstacles as opportunities and believes anything is possible with the right combination of creativity, hard work and perseverance. Applying this mindset has enabled Shannon to develop innovative solutions and stand out as a leader. In 2017, she founded encaptiv, an award-winning audience engagement platform for virtual, hybrid and in-person presentations and events.

Shannon is a TEDx Speaker and a 40 Under Forty award winner. She holds a master's degree in interpersonal communication from the University of Central Florida and has served on the faculty at Columbia University and Iona College. She is also cofounder of Stamford Innovation Week, a weeklong conference celebrating innovation, entrepreneurship and technology in Stamford, Connecticut.

Connect with Shannon:

Website: shannonmalkindaniels.com
LinkedIn: linkedin.com/in/shannonmalkindaniels
Twitter: @shannonmdaniels

Asking for Help is Not a Sign of Weakness

We begin asking for help the moment we are born. Think about it—as soon as you enter the world, you cry for help, literally. You exit the womb kicking and screaming, saying, "I'm here, and I'm HUNGRY. Feed me!" Nobody taught you to ask for help in that moment; you just inherently knew to do so.

As we grow and develop, we learn how to best ask for help. We evolve from crying as our only means of asking someone to change our diaper, feed us or give us our pacifier, to pointing, making noises and eventually forming words. Over time we discover what works and, perhaps more importantly, what does not.

For me, I quickly learned (okay, maybe not *that* quickly) as a young child that launching myself into the air, flopping on the floor, kicking and screaming did not work so well. Sure, it got me attention, but it did not get me what I really wanted or needed help with. Many times, this behavior resulted in punishment. Asking for help is a learning process. It takes some trial and error, but we eventually figure out the most effective ways to request assistance.

As we continue to grow, we are taught to be more and more self-sufficient—call it nature, nurture or a combination of the two. Regardless, we gradually go from peeing in our pants and asking our parents to change our Pull-Ups, to learning how to go to the bathroom on our own. And the older we get, the more we learn to do for ourselves.

Along the way, asking for help becomes something we do less and less. For some reason, as a society, we are conditioned to believe that asking for help is a sign of weakness. That if we cannot do something ourselves, we are somehow failing, not smart enough, not good enough, or not talented enough. But have you ever really stopped to ask why that is?

Maybe it is because some people think asking for help is a way of admitting, "I don't know it all." Well, guess what, reality check: You *don't* know it all. Nobody does. Unless, of course, you have downloaded the contents of the internet into your brain (which may not be that far off in the future), but even then, do you *really* know everything? And honestly, who would *want* to know everything? The world would be a pretty boring place with nothing left to discover. And even if you did know everything, it would not make you automatically good or even competent at everything. That is where asking for help comes in.

Asking for help is not a sign of weakness; it is quite the opposite. Asking for help is a sign of strength. Let's break it down:

- Strong people know they don't know everything.
- Strong people are not afraid to admit they need help.
- Strong people play to their strengths and look to others to help fill gaps in their weaknesses.
- Strong people know that working with others makes them stronger.

Now take the word strong in the previous statements and replace it with each of the following:

- Smart (i.e., Smart people know that working with others makes them smarter.)
- Successful
- Skilled

You see, when you can admit what you do not know, that's when you start to grow. Unfortunately, I did not always know or understand this. When I graduated from college, I felt like I could take on the world. I had a degree, landed a great job, got promoted quickly and received a lot of pats on the back. But as I ascended the corporate ladder, I started to feel less and less competent. There were even times where I felt lost as I took on new roles and responsibilities. Because I had been excelling so easily and rapidly in my career without asking for help, I figured that I could not start after I had been promoted. I told myself numerous stories to rationalize why I should not ask for help:

- *Leadership clearly thinks I know how to do the job, or they would not have given it to me.*
- *If I ask for help, it is going to look like I do not know what I am doing. I can handle the workload.*
- *I will just take it home and work 80 hours a week.*

But the longer I resisted asking for help, the more I started to feel burnt out. My growth—both personally and professionally—began to slow down. I was no longer getting a promotion every year or so; it was now taking more than two years to move up another rung on the ladder, or I was getting passed over altogether. I could not figure out why, so I started to look at how other people were moving forward in their careers. What were they doing that I was not? I knew I was intelligent, great at my job and exceeding my goals. What was missing?

The answer: I was not asking for help. I was trying to do everything myself and not delegating to (or trusting) others. Sure, I was doing a pretty damn good job, but just not as good as I could have done if I had simply asked for help from others.

After I had this epiphany, I immediately started doing some things differently. First, I started to keep a strengths and weaknesses list. Yes, I wrote down every strength and weakness I had. But I did not just do a self-assessment; I asked others to give me an honest evaluation of how they perceived my strengths and weaknesses. It was not easy to hear about my flaws, but it was incredibly enlightening and helped set me on a new trajectory to even greater success. I then revisited that list every six months to review it, update it and leverage it to improve myself.

The insights gained from this exercise not only showed me where I had skill deficits, it helped me to home in on what I was good at and enjoyed. And where most people would say, "Focus on improving your weaknesses," I took a very different approach. I decided to nurture my strengths, to become even better at what I was already good at. Of course, I worked on improving areas of weakness as well, but I did that by asking for help.

You see, the first step to being successful is admitting that you do not know everything. The second step is asking for help. We all have our own strengths and talents, and these are generally aligned with our interests. When you focus on what you are good at, where your strengths lie and what you are truly interested in, you will flourish. But when you try to do everything, you will flounder. Sure, maybe you will get by for a bit, but eventually your weaknesses will be unearthed, and you will end up doing more harm to your reputation than good. That is why it is important to focus on those things that enable you to prosper...and ask for help with everything else.

I learned the hard way that asking for help and getting something done right the first time is a much better option than having to do rework. It saves time and money and leads to better outcomes, and you become a rising star. And when you work with a dynamic team of people who have unique strengths and skillsets, especially those that fill your aptitude gaps, you achieve greater results together. You do not have to create a formal work group or team; it can simply be a group of your peers—people whom you rely on for help, and provide help to, when needed.

It is also important to keep in mind that it is your responsibility to request help. Whether it is help from peers, your boss, friends or family, people do not know you need help unless you ask. In all my years as a manager, I became fairly good at recognizing when someone from my team was struggling and would extend help to them. Most of the time, the employee was grateful that I noticed and happily accepted the assistance. However, there were times I had employees who would say they were fine and did not need help. When this happened, they would continue to grapple with their work. It led to poor job performance, dissatisfaction, a negative work environment for all and, eventually, that individual's failure. The bottom line is, it is important to admit and speak up when you need help. If you find yourself in an environment where asking for help is frowned upon, you may want to rethink your current situation.

Should you decide to follow a management track, it is imperative that you create a safe environment that invites employees to ask for help and not be embarrassed to do so. This leads to a high-functioning team and success not only for your employees, but for yourself, the department and the organization as a whole.

I worked hard to create this environment not only in my corporate life but also as a college instructor. I taught my students that asking for help was not a sign that they were not intelligent, but rather that it displayed strength and an eagerness to learn. In my experience, students who took advantage of office hours, stayed after class, emailed me or asked for help in some other way grasped the material better, earned higher grades and performed better overall in school.

Bottom line? You should not view asking for help as a weakness but rather as a way to grow, develop, learn and excel. If you want to be successful, ask for help, no matter how big or small the task. Sure, I can jump, stretch or use a chair to reach the top shelf in the kitchen, but why not ask my 6-foot-5 husband to grab it for me? I will tell you one thing for certain: Asking for help to reach things on high shelves has saved me numerous broken glasses, bumps and bruises.

* * *

Bio for Michelle:

Michelle Puzzo is an entrepreneur, author and physical therapist. She was born in Connecticut and graduated from the University of Connecticut in 1998 with her bachelor's degree in physical therapy. In 2017 she founded Puzzo Boys, LLC and began writing children's books. In 2019 Michelle cofounded UR Community Cares to virtually link neighbors to support each other during a time of need. In 2020 she became a member of ImpervaWear Co. to help supply more people with PPE. She is dedicated to helping others.

Connect with Michelle:

Email: michellepuzzo@urcommunitycares.org
Website: www.URCommunityCares.org
LinkedIn: linkedin.com/in/michellepuzzo

Get Help, Give Help

I chose my career in physical therapy because I wanted to help people. After initially contemplating the fields of physical therapy and social work as vehicles for my passion, the help of my benevolent mentor David Tiberio guided me toward physical therapy (PT). He was a professor at the University of Connecticut (UConn) and owned an outpatient clinic specializing in orthopedic PT. I became his student at UConn after being a part-time aide at his clinic, where I shadowed him and learned all aspects of the operation. I enjoyed getting to know the patients and enjoyed being able to help each of them.

Being blessed with a mentor who inspired me to do my best in college allowed me to secure hands-on job experience throughout my college training. At that time, PT majors were mandated to do multiple internships to gain the field experience that would be required after graduation. I had the confidence to do all of mine out of state in Central

Florida; Reno, Nevada; and Southern California. Each setting was different and each job was different, but one thing was constant: I had to ask for help to learn new skills.

Upon completion of my college degree, I was offered a permanent position with an employer with whom I did my last internship in California. Throughout the initial six months of my new job, I tapped my coworkers for their knowledge, skills and experience. Fortunately, they were all happy to help, remembering their own experiences fresh out of school. After about a year and a half, I was feeling torn between my job and moving back to Connecticut to be closer to family members who could use my support. Since I grew up and attended college in the same area, I wanted to see the rest of the U.S., but my heart was in New England, and I missed watching the seasons change!

I asked my parents for help. They were and still are my go-to guy and gal when I am making a big decision. They have always guided me with wisdom and encouragement to continue to grow. Eventually, I made my decision, and then I called my dad and said, "I think it is time for me to come home." I felt as if I was weak for wanting to go back to Connecticut and be with my family, but it was where I needed to be. My dad hopped on a plane to San Diego, and we then drove home cross-country together. During the therapeutic journey, he explained that for a young professional, there is wisdom in experimenting and exploring various positions to become familiar with a variety of work experiences. I realized my job-change decision was not letting him down (even though he had the same job for over thirty-five years!), and I would prove how committed I was to my professional growth.

In my daily work, my PT patients ask me for help—to build strength, gain better balance and play sports again. As I started treating patients directly in their own homes, they requested help in moving on and off a bed, showering after knee surgery, and on how to talk to their adult children about wanting to live alone.

My role changed from the person who asked for help from my mentor, my professors, my parents and my coworkers to being the person whom others asked for help. Wow! My passion to help others had a positive effect on vulnerable lives. The valuable purpose in my chosen work allowed me to flourish. I saw firsthand the profound impact one can have when you can give someone sound advice and support.

My experiences inspired me to create an opportunity for those who wanted to donate time, effort and companionship to assist those who needed help. In 2019, I cofounded UR Community Cares (UCC), a 501(c)(3) nonprofit community organization. We allow older adults and those with a physical disability to virtually ask for help from their neighbors, using a secure digital platform. Many people in this population can find it difficult to ask for help due to being the ones who usually are helping others. Our confidential website allows for registration and pairing of participants based on their needs, interests and location.

Many of our community members do not want to ask for help because they think it is a sign of weakness and feel their independence may be taken away. Pride and fear can sometimes get in the way of asking for help, but connecting with another human being when you need support the most will offer new perspectives. I think that many people overlook the fact that asking for assistance gives you access to another person's wisdom and a way to gain more independence in your future endeavors.

Life's experiences have brought me to this conclusion: We all need help. I made providing help my personal and professional mission. UCC has a secure and safe volunteer support program that virtually connects community members who need volunteer help with house or yard work, companionship and transportation. Our volunteers are dedicated to supporting their neighbors who want to remain independent in the comfort of their own homes.

In closing, I have enjoyed a fulfilling career in PT and launched a volunteer support nonprofit after learning how important it is to ask for help. So, if you find that you need advice and guidance in taking the next steps in your career, don't hesitate to seek out support. You can go to the library, head back to school, seek career advice, or go online and search the web. It's normal for graduates to be anxious about the future because it is outside of their control. In order to make the best decisions, pursue contacts in careers that interest you, talk to a career counselor and look for a mentor who is willing to help you.

Helping people learn how to ask for help is my mission. What is yours?

* * *

Activity: A Helping Hand

Activity created by Jessica Pare, founder of Alchemy Learning Solutions.

What fears do you have about asking for help in your personal or professional life?

_____

_____

_____

What is one tactic or practice introduced in this chapter that you would like to experiment with incorporating into your life?

_____

_____

_____

What are three things you could ask for help with today?

_____

_____

_____

How do you feel when you are able to help someone else?

_____

_____

_____

What are three types of help you could offer to someone else in your life?

_____

_____

_____

6

Learning is a Lifelong Process

You will hear from Nicole Baccaro and Holly O'Driscoll.

Bio for Nicole:

Nicole Baccaro is a proud New Englander. She was born and raised in Connecticut and currently lives in Hartford County. Nicole holds a Bachelor of Science in Business Administration degree from Bryant University and a Master of Business Administration degree from Central Connecticut State University.

She has experience in operations across many industries and has held some unique innovation roles. Nicole loves connecting with new people and building a sense of community in her area. Outside of work, you can find her spending time with friends, family and her dog, Buddy; practicing yoga; and taking weekend trips whenever possible.

Connect with Nicole:

LinkedIn: linkedin.com/in/nicolebaccaro/

Post-Grad Life

Most people leave college graduation feeling like the world is their oyster. I, on the other hand, left feeling like my world was ripped out from under me. I loved my little college bubble. I was used to living with the same people for four years, always having friends around, enjoying the lack of real adult responsibility and, most importantly, feeling comfortable in the structure of classes and semesters. Although I graduated *cum laude* and with a job secured, I had no clue what was in store for my early twenties.

Post-college life required major adjustments. There was no structure or midday naps, my parents became my roomies, and I suddenly began questioning everything I was doing. I felt completely lost and missed the path that college faithfully constructed for me semester after semester. I was suddenly an independent unit with no handbook on what to do or how to do it.

I wanted to share my post-graduate life story so others do not feel so alone. My earlier twenties were an immense time of reflection, and I was not prepared for the confusion that comes with a new chapter of life. As of this writing, I am seven years out of college, still in my twenties, and in awe of how much I have grown in a short amount of time. The amount of learning that occurs during this period of life is wild.

I do not like the phrase "know yourself," because to me, it comes with great responsibility and guilt if you feel as if you do not know who you are yet. I instead prefer the phrase "knowing what you like, and knowing what you don't." Most of this learning is not necessarily out of a book, but more from reflection and finding what "works" for you and only you. This is a time to be selfish and to start building a sturdier foundation as an adult.

Below are some aspects of life that I have broken down to make exploring your own new foundation a little less daunting.

Routines

Routines are the biggest learning aspect of all; they are the foundation of the foundation, if you will. A routine, in any form, is the structure of your day, week, month and year. A routine does not have to be set in stone or a list of rules to be followed. It is more a way to be aware of your personal priorities. For example, how many hours of sleep do you typically get? Do you pack your lunch the night before, or buy lunch every day? Are your weeks packed with activities, or is your schedule completely free? What kind of basic choices do you make to bring less chaos to your day? For me, I make my lunch most nights before bed, and I aim for eight hours of sleep with no screen time before hitting the pillow. I am still learning my weeknights should not be packed and in fact should be purposely free from time to time so I can relax and recharge.

Mental and Physical Health

Being thrown into the real world can bring changes to our mental and physical health. I experienced both types of changes because I did not prioritize my well-being. I worked in sales and traveled nonstop during the day while simultaneously doing a part-time MBA program at night. My body & mind were running on fumes. As the years passed, I learned how to prioritize exercise and mental health activities. Do not be afraid or embarrassed to seek out professional help to manage your stress and learn ways to better cope with big life changes. Additionally, surrounding yourself with a supportive network of friends, family and colleagues is a major key for success. As for exercise, there are plenty of options: Hit the gym or a yoga class, walk thirty minutes at lunch, or search YouTube for free classes.

Education

If it is not clear yet, I am someone who does well with some structure. I missed classes when I did not have them anymore, and I discovered

I really missed learning. I graduated with my undergrad degree in May 2014, and I enrolled in an MBA program in September 2014. I earned my MBA in 2017 and thought I was done with school forever. The joke was on me, because a few years later, I signed up for an online health and wellness class at a local community college simply because I wanted to learn about nutrition. You may be like me and truly like learning in a classroom-style setting, or you may be nothing like me and hate school. Either way, there are plenty of ways to broaden your educational experiences that are outside the typical box. You may enjoy learning by watching documentaries in the comfort of your home. If you need a creative outlet, look into a pottery or cooking class. Check into local colleges to see what classes they offer that have absolutely nothing to do with your day job and everything to do with your interests. Do you subscribe to any podcasts? The options of education outside of college are truly endless and worth exploring!

Career

It is perfectly normal to not know what you want to do when you grow up. I wish I had heard that while accepting my college diploma. Navigating a career as a young adult can be extremely overwhelming. You may take the first job you can get, and suddenly you are sitting in a cubicle wondering, *How did I get here, and where do I go from here?* Oh boy, have I been there, and some days I am still there.

When you have moments like this, it is important to do some self-reflecting on your likes and dislikes. What do you like about your role? What do you not like? Do you like your company? Describe your ideal job. This reflection can pave the way for your future. Knowing these aspects about your own personal preferences can steer you in a better direction to move and apply for jobs that align better with who you are and what you value.

I understand that life after graduation can be a trying time. I hope that the four aspects I discussed bring your own personal learning from overwhelming to enjoyable.

* * *

Bio for Holly:

Holly O'Driscoll is an industry expert in the field of design thinking and human-centered innovation. Throughout her twenty-plus-year career, Holly has built a reputation as a master human-centered innovation strategist, trainer and facilitator and has led programs in more than twenty countries. She is the former Global Design Thinking Leader at Procter & Gamble, where she led more than 250 workshops, often at the request of C-suite executives. She is the founder and CEO of Ampersand Innovation, LLC, a design thinking and human-centered innovation strategy consultancy.

Connect with Holly:

Email: holly@holly-odriscoll.com
LinkedIn: linkedin.com/in/holly-n-odriscoll

Learning Does Not Stop After Graduation

Walking across the podium on graduation day might give you the feeling that your days as a student are over and that your learning journey is complete. In reality, this couldn't be further from the truth. While your university studies may be over, your learning experience is just changing phases, moving from the academic and familiar to something less formal and tangible—one activated by the many personal and professional experiences yet to be.

There is a wonderful quote carved into the cornerstone of the Stanford University Graduate School of Business that reads, "Dedicated to the things that haven't happened yet, and the people who are about to dream them up." I get chills and tears spring to my eyes just about every time I think about this quote and when I share it with others. For me, it represents the possibility and potential that live within each of us—and to deliver on these, we must lean into what is possible, dream big and consciously unlearn some of the things that we've been educated, socialized and corporatized to believe are true. Let me unpack what learning to unlearn means.

From a very young age, we quickly learn that it is not okay to be wrong or to get something wrong. We learn that the person with the highest test grade, game score or number of toys wins. We learn that the world is designed in a way that asks us all to play a zero-sum game, one that has a winner and a loser. Unlearning this unfortunate and arguably success-limiting concept requires daily effort. This is particularly true if you were brought up in a highly competitive, Western, first-world culture. It also may just be the most important investment you make in yourself. Why does this matter so much? As an innovator and leadership consultant, and a coach to business teams on how to achieve better outcomes, becoming okay with failure and recognizing the need to try something new not once, not twice, but perhaps dozens or hundreds of times is so important. That is right—just when you think you have learned all you need to learn, it's time to start unlearning.

This is so important to developing a mindset of possibility, of stating and then challenging assumptions, of imagining what might be. This means you will inherently get things wrong and get them wrong often, but that does not mean there is something wrong with you. Let that sink in for a moment—getting something wrong does not mean there is something wrong with you. It is an enlightening truth, and one of the most important things to realize. When you acknowledge that many things you were taught are not serving you or others well, it is amazing how opportunities, and people, start to show up in your life that can step change your growth and development.

Continuing on the theme of unlearning, the idea that "you don't know what you don't know" is a concept that hopefully inspires ongoing humility and grace. I do not recall hearing this phrase until well into my twenties, and I surely didn't learn it in school. In a culture where the intellectual yardstick is focused on what you *do* know, becoming aware of all the things you do *not* know can sometimes be a hit to your confidence. However, I recommend looking at this as an opportunity to increase your curiosity and willingness to once again challenge assumptions and explore alternative points of view. Often our world is much bigger than we think it is, and taking a moment to think about all that we do not know is such a valuable exercise.

While exploring alternate points of view is important, taking time to learn about yourself is also critical and truly a lifelong journey. This is called building self-awareness. Becoming clear on what you are thinking, feeling, saying and doing in any given situation is critical to knowing how you are showing up to the world. In the work I do with teams on innovation and strategy, we often use a tool called an empathy map to unlock the stakeholder experience. This same tool can be used on ourselves to better understand our own experiences. Here is a real-life example of an empathy map that was generated during a workshop that I facilitated in 2019:

The empathy map is a simple 2-by-2 sketch, one you can draw anywhere, anytime. (You can try this yourself in the activity at the end of this chapter.) In addition to stakeholders, customers, clients or even family members, use the empathy map on yourself to better understand your own experiences and perspectives, along with the experiences and perspectives of others. That's right—this is not just a tool for professional life. This is a tool that can be used to improve relationships and cultivate understanding across all parts of life. The more you practice, the better you will be at using the tool in everyday business and life situations, including the ones you are facing yourself. Dialing into how your thoughts and feelings shape your behavior can help you understand how you show up to others and the impact you have, either intentionally or unintentionally.

These are all examples of why lifelong learning is essential, even when the learning is actually unlearning something that is not serving you well, learning to be okay with getting something wrong, and learning more about yourself. While these concepts are not traditionally taught in formal education environments, they are life skills that absolutely have the ability to expedite your development as a leader and set the stage for you to develop not only yourself but those around you as well. One question I often ask clients when I am approached to help them tackle a business problem is: "Are you open to discovery, or are you looking to validate an existing point of view, either yours or someone else's?" In a world that often says it is more important to be right than to be curious, it can be tempting to search for validation. This is the easy route. Do not fall into the trap—sit in the discovery space, lean into the discomfort and ask yourself three things:

- *What must be true for me to build my comfort level with getting something wrong?*
- *What do I need to unlearn?*
- *What do I need to learn about myself to unleash my potential and that of the people around me?*

Your learning experience is not over when you finish school; in fact, it is just beginning. Only now, you, your curiosity and your experiences are the teachers.

* * *

Activity: Empathy Map

Activity created by Holly O'Driscoll, founder of Ampersand Innovation, LLC.

The empathy map is a simple 2-by-2 sketch, one you can draw anywhere, anytime. Use this tool for yourself to better understand your own experiences and perspectives.

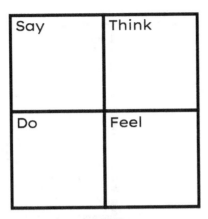

When completing an empathy map for self-awareness, consider the following points and use the answers to complete the map:

Reflect on a moment that is worthy of reexamination: a moment that perhaps went well, maybe a moment that did not go well, or perhaps it was so ordinary that you want to explore what happened there too—often it's in the small, uneventful moments that we can gain insight, as there's little emotion tied to these experiences.

What were you **SAYING** in this moment? What words did you literally use? What do you tell your friends about this moment or experience?

What were you **DOING** in this moment? What behaviors did you exhibit or enact? What actions did you take?

What were you **THINKING** in this moment? Spend a little time reflecting on your thoughts. What was driving you to think in this way? Was anything motivating you or holding you back?

How were you **FEELING** in this moment? Were you excited, worried, frustrated, or feeling any other emotions? If so, capture what you were excited about, worried about, etc.

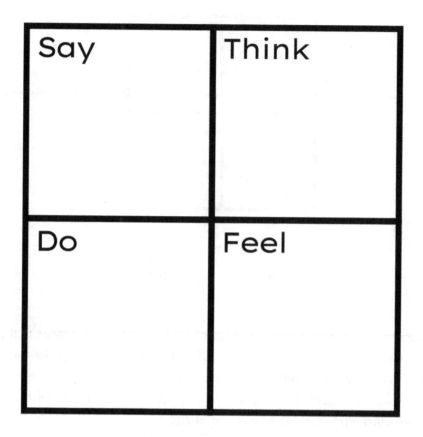

Now step back from your completed empathy map and reflect on the big picture. What are you learning about how you showed up? Was this result an intentional one? What might you do differently next time to show up in the way that you want? Do the exercise again at a different point in time and compare the two. What do you notice? What are you learning about yourself?

Remember, this exercise is about self-awareness, yet the same empathy map tool can be used to better understand your customer, your client, your boss, your new teammate, your in-laws (yes, it works in personal life too), and other stakeholders in your life.

7

Your Career Journey

You will hear from Joe Nespoli and Eric Consolazio.

Bio for Joe:

Joe Nespoli is a Sales Executive for New York Life Group Benefit Solutions. In Joe's first year in sales, he was the top selling sales representative in the country at his level. Prior to sales, Joe was the Product Manager for Cigna's Virtual Reality Meditation product and worked on a small skunkworks team under Cigna's CIO that supported the national account sales team in winning and retaining the top 1% of accounts. Joe is also a graduate of Cigna's Technology Leadership Development Program, a 3.5 year, IT rotational program where he worked across different Innovation teams in the U.S. and Glasgow, Scotland.

Joe recently obtained his MBA from the University of Hartford and he has an undergraduate degree from Temple University, where he served as Temple's mascot, Hooter the Owl.

Connect with Joe:

LinkedIn: linkedin.com/in/ josephnespoli/

There is No Right or Wrong Career Path

Throughout my entire life, I have always been obsessed with my future. I am always trying to plan my next move, role and goal. I would often ponder which steps I could take now that would catapult me into the future that I wanted.

The following is the advice I would give my younger self starting in my career, backed by the knowledge and experience I have now. Hopefully, it helps you!

When You are in Your First Job

When you are in your first job remember the following to try to stand out!

Set Big Goals

Write your goals down somewhere that is visible in your daily life. You cannot hit a bull's-eye if you are not aiming at one. Set large goals that almost seem unattainable. Break down the goal into daily, weekly and monthly tasks that will help you achieve it, and then get to work.

Put In the Work

Chances are, when you initially begin working in your first job, you are going to do tasks you have never done before, and you will have to learn new areas of business you may have only read about in class. Put in the work to master the subject areas. Positivity and aspirations will only get you as far as your hard work takes you.

Be Passionate

Go to work each day with a purpose. Have a strong "why" that is going to push you through the times that are a grind. Part of my "why" is to earn a lot of money so I can provide my parents with experiences I feel they deserve. They both worked in careers where they dedicated their lives to serving others, and they never made a ton of money. I want to take them on trips and treat them throughout their retirement. When I am putting in extra hours or dealing with a nightmare project or client, I have something pushing me beyond my paycheck.

Challenge Yourself

Back when I started doing improv, I was absolutely horrible at it. I was nervous and felt like I was always bringing down the rest of the improv team. The first few days of improv were torturous, but slowly I got better. Now as I work in sales, I might be asked a question I was not prepared for in a meeting or finalist presentation. The Joe before doing improv might have stumbled over his words and maybe lost the sale, but because of my experience with improv, I improved my ability to think on my feet. Improv also helped me get over the fear of rejection, as you constantly make mistakes when you are first starting out. Try to take on a stretch assignment or a project that you feel will push you to learn new things.

When You are in a Role You Don't Enjoy

Understand roles are not for life. You are never trapped. You can always pivot and change jobs or even careers. Do not stay unhappy—make moves.

"Someone's opinion of you does not have to become your reality." –Les Brown

This is one of my favorite quotes. It's important to believe in yourself even when others around you do not believe in you or see your vision. Use it as motivation and fuel for success. As much as my "why" has motivated me, the people who wrote me off or did not believe in me motivated me just as much. Remember, you can sometimes learn more from bad managers than good ones. They test you. Look for golden nuggets in each job that you can bring with you to future ones.

When I graduated from college, I used to puppy-sit and walk dogs to help pay off my student loans (outside of working my full-time job). When walking a dog, I soon noticed how a little puppy would affect people who looked miserable walking the streets—the sight of a dog would bring huge smiles to their faces. As silly as it may sound, I try to be like that dog in my sales role. When I go into an office, I see a group of individuals who are sometimes miserable and think this will be another boring insurance meeting. My goal is to bring smiles, laughs and joy to them during my meeting and to turn their day around. I want them to look forward to seeing me again. You can learn something from *every* job and *every* person. Pay attention!

When You are Trying to Change Jobs or Switch Careers

Identify ways you can gain experience for the job you want while in your existing position. I knew I wanted to pivot to sales about six months before I actually did. During that time, I thought about how I could practice selling in my current role in information technology. I began selling ideas and projects to the business and my manager. I was the product owner of a virtual reality product, and I began to think of ways to increase demand for the product and started tracking my success. I then was able to use those results as bullet points on my résumé when applying for sales positions.

Include Results, Not Just Responsibilities, on Your Résumé

This is a common mistake I see on a lot of résumés. Your job title should give the reader a good idea of what your responsibilities were. Your results are what can make you stand out from others.

Tailor Your Résumé to Each Job and Company

View the job description to see the responsibilities, qualifications and mission and values of the company you are applying to, and then tailor your résumé to match what the company wants. Not enough people do this, and it is an easy way to stand out. Use Fiverr to purchase a resume template or find a resume specialist.

Final Words...

Many of you are going to find out what you want to do by trial and error. The key is to enjoy the ride and always find things you appreciate—those golden nuggets—in each of your roles. Keep your eyes open for the people whose job you would like one day, and reach out to them to start building a relationship. See if they will be your mentor. Try to model the traits they have that will help bring you to the next level.

Please remember when you are not enjoying a role that you are never stuck. You can always switch jobs and companies, so keep your head up and be thankful you have a job! Take the steps needed for a career or job change and to better yourself.

The daily steps you take to improve yourself, along with your hard work, perseverance and a positive attitude no matter what you are faced with, are going to make you unstoppable.

Remember, there is no right or wrong career path.

* * *

Bio for Eric:

Eric Consolazio is a former Chief Information Officer (CIO) and senior technology executive. He was the CIO of Gartner, Inc., as well as Senior Vice President of Cigna's Global Customer Solutions Group. He was the creator of myCigna.com and managed the applications for the web, call center, mobile, social media and Cigna's Enterprise SOA services.

Eric was named the technology leader of digital innovation at Cigna, and in 2012, the company was recognized by InformationWeek as one of the top ten innovative companies for its online tools. In 2016, Eric was a keynote speaker at the Samsung Developer Conference, which was viewed by millions worldwide. He is a well-known speaker at industry forums, and his work has been referenced in numerous publications. Most recently, Eric has been immersed in the film industry as an executive producer.

Eric has a Master's degree in Finance and International Business from New York University, and a Bachelor's degree in Business Administration from Pace University.

Connect with Eric:

LinkedIn: linkedin.com/in/erixxcor

Choosing Your Career

Let's be clear right off the bat: I am not the person you should aspire to be. I also do not have the magic elixir in the bottle for you. I will leave that for others to sell you.

Why? Because we are all different. There is no one answer, even for you. You will need to make your own career choices along the way. Go right? Go left? Change lanes? There will be a series of decisions throughout your life that you will need to make. Your success will be determined by your ability to see an opportunity and to accept change while it is your choice, not when a metaphorical gun is put to your head.

Some believe that very successful people have better luck than others. Maybe that is true for some, but I believe the "luck" is:

- Having a career goal (which will probably change over time, but that is okay);
- Identifying opportunities...at the right time;
- Maximizing your strengths while teaming up with others;
- Building your reputation and personal credentials;
- Finding your personal work/life balance.

Having a Career Goal

Setting a personal goalpost is essential to having direction in life (Just think how pointless football would be without a goal). Having a goal helps you focus on opportunities to get you to where you want to go. Opportunities are your stepping-stones.

Setting a career goal should not fill you with anxiety, because it will invariably change over time. You see, the search for opportunities—the very things you need to achieve your goals—will also be the very thing that changes your goals. Your experiences will lead you in different directions; but that is okay, for it is your unique personal journey.

For example, I started college intending to become an accountant. I changed majors twice and graduated with a marketing degree. I later earned a Masters' degree in finance. I ended up having a successful career in information technology. Go figure.

Identifying Opportunities

Racehorses have blinders, which keep them focused. But you are not a horse. If your career is about solely wanting to take your boss's job and doing what he or she does, you are wearing blinders. Do not just compete to do other people's jobs. Find the gap between what other people are doing. Make connections that are missing and needed. Then become the expert. Trust me, there is a lot of gray space out there if you look for it. Gray spaces are transitory; they are gaps caused by change. That is why timing is important. It is better to be early than late; while many times frustrating, it is better to be ahead than behind in timing. Grasp the opportunities in the gray space created by change, and you become a change agent. It will be uncomfortable, at least at first, but do not let that deter you.

If what you do creates value and makes other peoples' lives better and easier, you have found your opportunity. Conversely, if you put an unrewarded burden on others, you will fail.

Personal example: I know I am hopelessly dating myself, but when I first started out in IT, mainframes were the center of the universe. I quickly realized I would never be better at mainframe computing than others around me. I saw a small beige IBM PC languishing in a corner. PCs were new at that time, and this PC sat there unused because it was still unfamiliar. I became curious, and then I became the expert. Later I saw the use of the internet as an opportunity to rapidly develop and deploy applications immediately worldwide, which was an otherwise arduous process back then. I became one of the experts in my industry in web-based development. I was not a genius; I just saw the opportunity, the place where others were not. It took me on a wild and wonderful ride.

In taking the initiative to fill gaps caused by change, sometimes you have to ask for permission, sometimes you quietly expand your responsibility, and sometimes you just have to declare.

Personal example: As I was heading up web development, the technologies for mobile and social media were new and evolving rapidly, but there was no formal IT development team in place at my company. We did not have experts, but we had smart people willing to take it on. We took the initiative and announced that we would become the company's center of excellence. It was hard work to achieve that, but it paid off.

Maximizing Your Strengths While Teaming Up with Others

Everyone has strengths and weaknesses, and your career should play to your strengths. Why team up with others? Your weaknesses are other peoples' strengths. People with different backgrounds and experiences working together provide a complete picture. Diversity is strength. Your success is not just in building your own career, but others' as well. The strength of your personal network is not how charming you are; it is in how much value you bring to others. Also remember, in order to move upward, you must develop the replacement for your current job. Succession planning is about putting yourself out of a job so that you have personal room to expand.

There is the saying "Do what you love." However, I have seen more than one person who has thrown themselves into their weakness, which happens to be what they love. I cannot draw but would love to be a painter. I would starve. Therefore, I would say it differently: "Find what you are good at and make it your passion." This will be an iterative process, and that path will be different for each person.

Building Your Reputation and Personal Credentials

Woody Allen once said, "Most of success in life is just showing up." What he meant was you need to be dependable. I would say, "Most of the success in life is finishing what you started." So many people start and do not finish; they bounce around for the quick career jump. Trust me, that will eventually catch up with you, stall your career and possibly force you to backtrack—not fun. Make a commitment, fulfill it, and build your credibility and expertise. That is how you become valuable to others, which is the key to a good career.

Finding Your Personal Work/Life Balance

There is an old saying: "You get out of it what you put into it." While this is a true statement, it says nothing about happiness. I was a crazy workaholic for most of my career and travelled extensively. It was great money and great for my career, and I enjoyed it, but I missed some things in life that I will never be able to get back.

Everyone's balance is different. Family, friends and other pursuits that may fulfill you have to be factored into the equation. Work/life balance will also change over time as your life evolves. It is not one big decision; it is a thousand small decisions that add up over time. You may at some point have to revise your career goals, but if your life inside *and* outside of work ultimately makes you happy and fulfilled, you will have found your personal work/life balance.

Some Final Thoughts

Life and the environment around us are constantly changing. To deny that is to spit into the wind. Everyone has the ability to adapt, but their desire to adapt differs greatly. You can decide to 1) Accept change and progress; 2) Resist change and fall back; or 3) Seek opportunity through change and excel. I literally started at the bottom rung of the career ladder. Change became my friend. While others cringed at disruption, I saw opportunity. It paid off.

Some additional points to keep in mind:

- Bad decisions can be corrected;
- Good decisions today will not last forever;
- Expect the unexpected;
- Embrace change;
- Diversity is strength.

Finally, remember your career is a marathon, not a sprint. It will take most of your lifetime to finish your career journey. It will be difficult at times. Learn from the successes and mistakes. Know that it will be rough at times climbing the mountain, but at the end, you will enjoy the view.

* * *

Activity: Create a Career Map

To understand where you want to go, it is important to first document where you have been. From there you can identify possible next steps in your career journey. Start by documenting what you enjoyed about your roles.

Past role: _____

What did you enjoy about the role?

_____
_____
_____

Past role: _____

What did you enjoy about the role?

_____
_____
_____

Past role: _____

What did you enjoy about the role?

_____
_____
_____

Current role: _____

What do you enjoy about the role?

_____
_____
_____

Looking forward into the future, there could be multiple directions you take with your career. There is no right or wrong answer. Identify several potential next steps you may be interested in taking in your journey as well as what you may need to accomplish these goals.

Potential role: _____

What steps must you take to move into this role?

_____

_____

_____

Potential role: _____

What steps must you take to move into this role?

_____

_____

_____

Potential role: _____

What steps must you take to move into this role?

_____

_____

_____

8

Risk-Taking in Your Twenties

You will hear from Luis A. Valdez-Jimenez and Christine Schindler.

Bio for Luis:

Luis A. Valdez-Jimenez, Esq., MBA, earned his Bachelor of Arts in Political Science degree from Florida International University and then earned his Juris Doctor and Master of Business Administration degrees from the University of Wisconsin-Madison. During his career, he has held positions of increasing responsibility in aviation and technology companies converting legal risks into business opportunities. Luis is also passionate about serving on nonprofit boards, and he currently serves on the board of directors for 360 Federal Credit Union and previously for local chapters of Prospanica and United Way. In 2021, he launched ECLPS360, a Language Ventures Company, a firm that helps businesses overcome language barriers (ECLPS360.com).

Connect with Luis:

LinkedIn: linkedin.com/in/luisvaldezjimenez

The Cross-Country Gamble

It was the spring of 2015, and I was preparing to finish my dual Juris Doctor and Master of Business Administration degrees at the University of Wisconsin-Madison in my mid-twenties. In the previous fall, I had interviewed with several companies about post-graduation employment opportunities, and I was offered a job by a subsidiary of Raytheon Technologies Corporation (RTC) based in Connecticut. It seemed like my dream job and a dream industry I wanted to excel in, so I was excited. However, I quickly realized that I knew nothing about Connecticut, I had never even been there before my job interviews, and I knew literally no one who lived there except for the people I had interviewed with. How would I meet people? How would I know what issues people care about? How would I be noticed and advance in my career without the help of an established network? I had to admit, I was intimidated, and I debated whether to take the job. However, I decided to take the gamble and move to this completely unknown place. It was one of the best decisions of my life.

My situation was not unique. Many people need to take a daring leap of faith by moving to a new place in order to establish themselves in the careers, companies and industries they are interested in. The twenties are a great time to make such bold moves, as you are often single, do not have kids, and do not have a house or condo tying you down somewhere. Plus, if the move does not work out, there is still plenty of time to move on somewhere else.

I was fortunate enough to receive my job offer several months before I graduated, so I had some time to prepare. Even if you are presented with a sudden or unexpected opportunity, my first suggestion is to research the new location online before you arrive. Social media sites like Facebook and Meetup are great ways to find events and groups of people with similar interests. While I certainly wanted to make new friends, I also wanted to find out which groups could help me build a network. I recommend you search for young professional and industry organizations you are interested in and join their mailing lists and social media pages ahead of time to see the types of activities they engage in and the kinds of people who are involved. If you graduated from a university or college, see if there is an alumni group in the area you are moving to.

Right after I moved to Connecticut, I began to attend young professional events. I met someone, who also worked for RTC and who eventually became a great friend and mentor to me. He recommended that I join the Emerging Leaders Society, an official young professionals' affinity group of the United Way of Central and Northeastern Connecticut. I also joined the local chapter of Prospanica, the association of Hispanic professionals. These were exactly the kinds of organizations I wanted to join and volunteer with because they provided me with the opportunity to give back (something I have always been passionate about), network with other ambitious professionals, and get to know the area.

I suggest you not only volunteer but take advantage of the youthful energy and ambition you have in your twenties to step it up and serve in a leadership role within one of these local organizations. Often when you are young and right out of school, your employer may be reluctant to give you leadership opportunities at work. Instead of being passive and waiting for leadership to come to you, be proactive and seize the leadership opportunities many local nonprofit organizations and boards have. I eventually became chair of the Emerging Leaders Society and president of the Connecticut Chapter of Prospanica, which benefited me in numerous ways. I began to cut my leadership teeth in these organizations, and I began getting noticed by local awards programs, media outlets and other important and influential people. After being recognized in the *Hartford Business Journal*'s 40 Under Forty Awards, a senior executive at another RTC division reached out and offered me the opportunity to meet him. Eventually, I got a major promotion to move to that RTC division!

In summary, if you are going to a new place where you do not have many contacts, I suggest developing a plan for mitigating your risks of not breaking in. Do your research on local organizations and groups you may be interested in. When you arrive, join them and take on a leadership role. You will find that you will soon develop an impressive network of powerful and ambitious people not just within your own company but others as well, you will get to know the area quickly, and your leadership skills will develop in a way that will help you get noticed and advance in your career faster than if you did not become involved.

I recently returned home to South Florida to be closer to family, and I am actively employing these tactics I developed in Connecticut (along with utilizing prior relationships). Not only did I move, but also launched my own startup, ECLPS360. Moving no longer scares me, and nor should it scare you!

* * *

Bio for Christine:

Christine Schindler is an engineer and entrepreneur passionate about utilizing technology to overcome gaps in our world. Witnessing the gap in gender representation in STEM fields, she founded the non-profit organization Girls Engineering Change (GEC), which brings college students and middle school girls together at college campuses across the country to build low cost devices which are donated to organizations across the world, demonstrating the impact engineering can have on our communities. She then founded PathSpot, a technology company of which she now serves as CEO, with technology she invented to to instantly detect carriers of harmful contamination that commonly spread through poor handwashing. PathSpot is used by restaurants, packaging facilities, and farms to encourage sanitation practices, protect our food supply, and create a healthier world. Christine's work has been recognized by Forbes 30 under 30, Fast Company's World Changing Ideas, and Time Magazine's Best Inventions.

Connect with Christine:

LinkedIn: linkedin.com/in/christine-schindler11/

Betting on Yourself

"Aerodynamically, the bumblebee shouldn't be able to fly, but the bumblebee doesn't know it, so it goes on flying anyway." –Mary Kay Ash

While this quote is not scientifically true, it captures my opinion on the value of risk-taking in your twenties, before you have the chance to evolve and develop the experience to know whether something is (or is not) possible. One of my lab research professors in college told me her favorite students to work with were undergraduates because she could give them lab projects and problems that more experienced PhD and master's degree students would deem "impossible" based on their knowledge and experience. Without any preconceived ideas of what was possible or not, the undergraduate students would figure out how to solve them.

The stories of the bumblebee and of the lab students are echoed throughout all areas of life and encapsulate why I love being an "under-experienced" founder, entrepreneur, CEO and inventor.

I decided to take a risk in my twenties because I was passionate about a real problem I saw in the world—a problem creating illness and harm. No one else was solving this particular problem, and I felt there was a world-changing opportunity in deciding to do so. Even though I was enjoying and excelling in my job at the time, I thought the idea of working on a real problem no one else was tackling would make a bigger impact on the world.

After this realization, I quit my job, sold my car, and bought a 3D printer. I got to work inventing a solution, and in the following months deployed it across the country. I also raised venture capital to build and support a team that would be able to carry this mission forward faster and change the narrative around the problem we were solving.

The benefit of doing all of this in my twenties was that I took on the role of the bumblebee. I did not know if it was possible, so I decided that it was. My lack of experience allowed me to enter conversations and new environments with open eyes, which helped me identify gaps and create opportunities from what was missing. What I lacked in experience I compensated for with hustle, power, drive and passion. I also acknowledged what I did not know and built a network of experts, mentors and supporters to lean on when I needed help in areas where I lacked experience. I shared my energy and passion for this problem with my team and my supporters, which created a powerful force for change.

Had I been older or more established in my career, I do not think I would have approached this problem in the way that I did. As I have grown and developed an idea into an invention and then into a company recognized by industry leaders across the world, many people have told me my idea could not, should not or would not work. But by recognizing the trends in those conclusions, I felt only more empowered to work through them. The fresh perspective I brought to this problem gave me courage to solve it in the first place. If I had known what this path would look like, I do not know if I would have ever started down it. However, I did not know, so I started, and now each day I wake up and take as many steps down the path as I possibly can, empowered by the ability to make a difference.

Risk-taking at any stage in your life can be daunting. However, I believe with risk, when channeled in the direction of something that matters to you, can create a lasting change not only in your life but in the world around you.

An entrepreneur and leader of a unicorn start-up valued at over $1 billion once told me, "I think being an entrepreneur is actually the least risky path you can take, because you are betting on yourself."

Whether betting on yourself to start a business, put yourself up for a promotion, switch to a job with more unknowns, or challenge yourself in another aspect of your life that is considered a risk, I have found that by betting on yourself and taking the risk, you are able to see the positive impact of that risk more clearly. By pushing and challenging yourself, you may fail, but you will learn and grow infinitely faster because of the experience.

One of my favorite parts of taking this risk in my twenties has been that I know I will now challenge myself to risks for the rest of my life. I have tangibly seen what the benefits of taking the "risky" path can be and the opportunity that comes from betting on yourself. I would challenge everyone to take risks as early as you can in your career to develop the habit. You will find that risk-taking leads to transcending one challenge after another and creates ripple effects for a lifetime.

* * *

Activity: Identify One Career Risk You Want to Take in Your Twenties

What is it?

_____

_____

_____

_____

Why do you want to do it?

_____

_____

_____

_____

If you don't do it now, could you do it later?

_____

_____

_____

Who can help you make it happen?

_____

_____

_____

9

Your Personal Brand

You will hear from Christina Musto and Stacey Ross Cohen.

Bio for Christina:

Christina Musto is a third-generation wine grape broker at Musto Wine Grape Company, home winemaker, and certified sommelier (WSET II), with a Master's in Wine Business degree from Sonoma State University. She is a longtime member of the American Wine Society and a co-founder of the Women Winemakers of New England, and she works at Musto Wine Grape Company in Hartford, Connecticut, as Head of Sales, Marketing, and Winery Consulting. Christina is passionate about all things wine, winemaking, helping others start their own wineries, and supporting female-run beverage businesses by promoting them on social media and sharing her hands-on experience and expertise in the field. Christina also has a personal wine blog and writes for *WineMaker* magazine, the *American Wine Society Journal*, and CTVisit.com if she's not geeking out about wine or spending time with family and friends.

Connect with Christina:

Website: juicegrape.com
Instagram: @mustowinegrapeco
Website: threadsandvino.net
Instagram: @threadsandvino

10 Tips to Personal Branding Success

When done right, a personal brand can look easy to launch and effortless to maintain, but there is no special sauce or hack that comes with creating your own personal brand. What it really comes down to is if you are willing to put in the hard work and have the passion and commitment to stick it out through thick and thin to reap the rewards of having a successful personal brand.

Personal branding is personal. You need to get clear on why you want to do this. For me, it is not all about being a brand. My personal brand is a combination of personal, professional and intrinsic motivation. I personally love wine and the wine industry; it is something that I could talk about for hours, days, weeks...how much time do you have? Professionally, I help run my father's business, which is centered on wine grapes, winemaking, and start-up wineries. As in any small or family-run business, you end up "being the brand" by default. These days, the public wants to know the story behind the product, and that "story" is what I try to give my customers every day. Finally, I intrinsically love helping people with their businesses, especially female-run businesses. There was not (and still is not) a lot of female representation in the wine industry, and I'm always excited to share their stories with my audience.

So, what is your "why?" What lights you up? What do you want to put out into the world? Why are you creating a personal brand? Figure it out, write it down, and get working. The tips below should help get you started:

1. Decide what you want to be known for.

What inspired you to do this? What do you want to share with the world? Having this in the forefront of your mind will make creating content much easier. You will know where your focus should be and not waste time.

2. Identify your target audience.

Whom do you want to attract? Where do they hang out online and in the world? What are you bringing to the table that they cannot get elsewhere? You need to know whom you want to reach and be laser-focused. Get insanely detailed about your target demographics: Who are they? How old are they? What are their interests? How much money do they earn? Are they professionals or students? What are their likes and dislikes? What struggles are they facing, and how are you helping them? This will help when creating content and marketing towards your target audience. The more you know about your target audience, the more you will be able to bring them value. Putting in the work now will help you avoid spinning your wheels and wasting time in the future.

3. Develop a mission statement for your brand.

A mission statement describes the values and goals of your brand. It will help keep you focused when setting up your brand. What is your brand about? Keep it simple and straightforward. For example, my personal blog threadsandvino's mission statement is "To inspire and encourage women to create wine brands they love while having fun and enjoying life with family and friends." Simple, concrete, and to the point. The more targeted your mission statement, the better.

Your mission statement can change at any time. This is *your* personal brand. I have adjusted my mission statement many times because my business is always evolving. The great thing about having your own brand is that you have complete control over it. It will change and grow, just like you change and grow.

4. Build a website.

Even if you are on every social media platform, you still need a website. Having a website is a signal to people that they can trust you and that you are serious about what you're putting out there. Depending on the style of your brand, you could use it as a virtual résumé, create an online store, share resources with your followers, and more! There are so many inexpensive options that you can use. Get something simple set up and move forward.

5. Create social media channels.

When setting up your social media channels, refer back to your target audience. Figure out which social media platforms they are on and start there. Social media can be overwhelming, but I focus on the top three places—Facebook, Instagram, and wine forums—my target audience is on, and I put my time and energy there. If I tried to post content on all of the different platforms out there, I would not be able to keep up. If I am able to hire a social media staff member in the future, I may consider expanding my reach. But if you are just starting out, and it is just you, do not overwhelm yourself. It will just slow you down.

6. Be authentic.

People are very good at picking up on whether others are being authentic or not. That is probably part of the reason you are starting your personal brand. I know part of the reason I started mine was because there were so many "wine experts" recommending wine who did not know the difference between Cabernet and Merlot! When you are authentic, you create integrity and build trust with your audience. That is more important than the number of followers you have. Authenticity creates a loyal following and genuine engagement with your brand. Make sure to be true to yourself and your audience. People want to connect with the real you.

7. *Network with people in your realm.*

Whom do you look up to? What is it about them that makes you want to follow or network with them? Think about the qualities these people have that you admire and try to mirror them and learn from them. Even if it is someone who is far outside of your networking circle (such as a well-known motivational speaker), there is always something to learn from others. If you do have access to someone you admire, reach out to them and offer to buy them coffee and pick their brain, go visit their businesses if you can, or interview them for your blog or podcast. Celebrate them, learn from them, network with them, and become your own successful version.

8. *Consider hiring a business coach.*

When you are starting out or trying to expand your brand, it can be very helpful and productive to bounce ideas off of a business coach, especially if the industry you are in is not very collaborative. These professionals help you organize your thoughts and take the next steps in your business. Surrounding yourself with good people is vital, and an effective business coach can help your brand skyrocket! If you have the means, hiring a coach is worth the investment.

9. *Find a good business lawyer.*

It is always good to be prepared when it comes to legal situations. I suggest finding a good lawyer to help you set up all of your legal business requirements so you are protected. They can help with trademarks, protecting your intellectual property and products, and, heaven forbid, if someone tries to sue you. You are putting time and energy into your brand, and the bigger and more successful you are, the more exposed you are. It is smart to make sure you that you and your brand are protected.

10. Create and maintain a budget.

Create an initial budget and keep track of how much money you are spending. Knowing what you spend and what you earn can help you better plan for a variety of business expenses and opportunities that may come your way. Many people launch personal brands with the goal of transitioning them into full-time jobs. If this is a goal for you, once you have an idea of what you need to spend and earn to grow your business, you can start to map out when you can quit your full-time job.

Having a rainy day fund for your business is helpful as well—you never know if you are going to need advice from your lawyer or be presented with a once-in-a-lifetime opportunity that requires a decent amount of cash to make it happen.

And, lastly, invest in yourself. This could include taking a class to gain some insight on a certain topic or hiring a business coach. You want to have funds available to you so you can create the best and most valuable content.

Now that you have a decent road map, it is time to get going! Put your content out into the world! Video, photos, blog posts, articles, items for sale—anything to get the ball rolling on your personal brand.

If you are overwhelmed, break it all down into small steps. Small steps taken equal forward momentum. Be curious. Trust yourself. Be gentle with yourself. But above all, PUT IN THE TIME and DO THE WORK.

* * *

Bio for Stacey:

Stacey Ross Cohen has been studying the personal branding approach of students, job seekers and CEOs for decades. An award-winning marketing professional who earned her stripes on Madison Avenue and at major television networks, Stacey is a sought-after speaker and author in the realm of personal branding. She is cofounder of College Prime, a platform which helps college-bound students cultivate, perfect and activate their personal brands to become tomorrow's leaders. In 1997, Stacey founded Co-Communications, a full-service public relations and marketing agency serving clients in education, health care, real estate, professional services, and the nonprofit realm. Stacey excels at taking brands to market—she leverages each client's unique voice to make an indelible impact on social media, in board rooms, and everywhere in between. She has garnered the Forbes Enterprise and PRSA Practitioner of the Year awards for her work in the field. A staple at industry conferences, Stacey recently made her debut on the TED stage and is a blogger at the Huffington Post and Thrive Global and has been featured in *Entrepreneur, Forbes, Crain's, Sales & Marketing Management,* and a suite of other national media. She holds a Bachelor of Science in Human Development from Syracuse University and an MBA from Fordham University, and she recently completed a certificate program in Entertainment, Media & Technology at NYU Leonard Stern School of Business.

Connect with Stacey:

Facebook: facebook.com/StaceyRossCohen
LinkedIn: linkedin.com/in/staceycohen2
Instagram: @staceyrosscohen
Twitter: @StaceyRossCohen

Getting an Early Start to Personal Branding

Personal branding entails differentiating oneself from the competition to ultimately help you achieve college placement, career success, personal success, thought leadership, or even celebrity status. Personal branding requires the honing of one's narrative to establish an identity, which is then amplified through social media and other channels.

Our individual brands define who we are in the workforce—they guide our career paths, and they have an indelible impact on our financial future. In short, they're one of the most important aspects of professional life. Although it may seem that brands "just happen," building brand equity is not an overnight process. Personal branding should start early, allowing the brand to grow and strengthen over time. The ideal time to start is high school. High school is when personal brands first meet a larger audience: college admissions counselors, athletic coaches, future professors, and others. Teens should identify and hone their strengths and interests—a clear, powerful brand can land a student at a top college and entice prospective employers.

Readying for the often-dreaded college admissions process has changed dramatically. College admissions are no longer based solely on test scores, transcripts and essays. More and more, what teens post online influences the college admissions process. In fact, findings from a recent American Association of Collegiate Registrars and Admissions Officers (AACRAO) survey indicates that approximately 75 percent of admissions officers monitor applicants' social media as part of the admissions decision-making process.

What tips the balance these days is "identity" and "character." When students don't use good judgement, the consequences are dire. Consider Harvard University's 2017 withdrawal of admission offers to ten incoming freshmen for offensive Facebook posts. Harvard's decision created a stir and serves as an eye-opener for students, parents and college admission officers alike. It's now clear that what happens online matters offline, too. These students were able to make Harvard's 4.59 percent acceptance rate—but lost it all because of poor social media behavior.

Below are seven tips for getting started:

1. Strong brands are intentional.

Start by defining yourself. Determine what you do well, what you love to do, and your identity and vision. Then own it. This all starts with a self-audit to pinpoint your purpose, strengths, values and passion. It's essential to crystallize your uniqueness—or, competitive advantage—and why you're a worthy investment. Equally important is understanding your audience: what they need, how they function and what drives them to take action.

2. Have an answer to the question, "What's in it for me?"

Why should your target audience employ you? What's your value? What makes you stand out from the host of other applicants? You need to stress your value and strengths.

3. Know how to work a room.

Networking is face-to-face marketing. Don't focus on how many people you meet networking—focus on meeting the right people. Building relationships is the core of effective networking.

4. Stay on brand.

Maintain a consistent voice across different channels. Ensure your LinkedIn, Twitter and other profiles are up-to-date and in harmony.

5. Be self-aware.

Always seek feedback. Ensure your brand is not only clearly articulated, but also that you know how to deliver on your brand and make it grow.

6. Create a powerful online presence.

Reputation management is key. The digital footprint you leave across the internet is the encapsulation of your personal brand.

7. Have a multichannel approach.

Your toolkit should include, but not be limited to: LinkedIn, blogging, volunteer work and more. Consider all touch points, like email and mailed greetings. To stand out, develop a résumé with keywords and customized infographics. College-bound students should create a LinkedIn professional profile around age 16 and start engaging with colleges of interest.

For many, college admission is the first big test of your personal brand. If you want a ticket to lifelong success, nothing beats a degree from a top university—and teens today are keenly aware of that fact. Most are equally aware just how tough getting through that college gate has become.

Let's pause and talk about reputation. As aptly put by Jeff Bezos, founder of Amazon, "Your brand is what other people say about you when you're not in the room." At the foundation of any personal brand is a singular and paramount trait: our reputations. Without a positive reputation, no personal brand can flourish. If you're not viewed as a dependable and trustworthy professional, your skill set, interests and output—no matter how impressive—won't matter much.

Due to the amount of personal data online, managing online reputations is no longer optional, nor should it be an afterthought. The internet, in many ways, remains a Wild West. As a result, it's up to individuals to ensure their reputations remain sterling.

Here are several ideas for making your personal brand shine.

Maintain a squeaky-clean online profile.

If someone Googles your name, what photo of you do they see? Even a superficial scan may reveal things you don't want seen: racist or sexist comments, bullying, photos with a red Solo cup, evidence of drug use and more. The earlier you realize that prudence is your best policy online, the stronger your personal brand will be.

Seek out and engage mentors.

Use the same online tools you spend for socializing to reach out to people who are into things that intrigue you. You will often find that people in exalted positions are surprised and delighted to get questions from people who are interested in their professions. When it comes time to apply for a job, you may find those same people are happy to assist you.

Step up and volunteer.

Many schools now require students to do a certain number of volunteer hours as part of their curriculum. And if you already have career aspirations in a certain direction, this is a great way to get a head start. If you want to be a doctor, seek out volunteer opportunities to work with children with differing abilities in a long-term care facility.

Deliver on your promise.

Remember: You are the product. Gauge your brand behavior and ensure you return phone calls and emails promptly. Not delivering on promises can wreak havoc on the integrity of your personal brand.

These are just some of the key aspects of how skillful personal branding can help you get over the greatest obstacle of your young life. None of it is rocket science, just careful and deliberate steps required to reach the goal.

* * *

Activity: Starting Your Personal Brand

Activity created by Stacey Ross Cohen, CEO and President of Co-Communications.

Create your mission statement. What is your vision and purpose?

_____

_____

_____

_____

_____

What are your values and passion? (*Consider your belief system and operating principles that drive you.*)

_____

_____

_____

Do a self-assessment of your top brand attributes. *Think of four adjectives that best describe the value you offer or words that describe your personality (examples: collaborative, ambitious, risk-taker, creative).*

Brand Attributes:

1. _____

2. _____

3. _____

4. _____

What are your core strengths or functional skills? *Hint: Think of responsibilities that you excel at, what things make you that go-to person (examples: solution-oriented, delegating, innovating, managing conflict, fact-finding, writing).*

_____
_____
_____
_____
_____

How are you currently communicating with key audiences?

_____
_____
_____

What resources are you currently using to execute your personal branding program?

_____

_____

How much time do you currently allocate to personal branding efforts?

_____

_____

What additional untapped resources do you have access to?

_____

_____

_____

Outline three quantifiable goals for your personal branding program. *Make sure they are "SMART" (Specific, Measurable, Actionable, Realistic, Timely) goals. Consider short- and long-term goals.*

_____

_____

_____

_____

_____

_____

Who is your competition in the marketplace and what differentiates you from them? *Determine why decision makers should choose what you're of-fering over others offering similar value. What makes you the best choice? What makes you a good investment?*

_____

_____

_____

_____

Who is your target audience? *(Hint: Think of where you want to fit in—industry/niche of expertise.) Find out where decision makers in that field "hang out" and what they perceive as the "it" factor. Then position yourself in front of them and capture their attention.*

_____

_____

_____

_____

What do you want to tell people?

_____

_____

_____

_____

_____

_____

What do you want them to do with that information?

_____

_____

_____

_____

What is the desired outcome?

_____

_____

_____

_____

_____

10

The Power of Philanthropy

You will hear from Stephanie Wagner and Mike A. Williams.

Bio for Stephanie:

Stephanie Wagner is a real estate agent who has been selling homes for twenty-two years. She truly loves helping people find their dream home, but she also feels her heart still belongs in the classroom. She has a double degree in special education and elementary education from Boston University.

Before she started her own family, Stephanie developed two state and federal educational programs. The first program was for the Stonington, Connecticut, public school system. The second program was based in Vernon, Connecticut, but actually serviced multiple towns. Stephanie also ran a private nursery school for seven years. Having a positive impact on children has been the most rewarding part of her life.

Connect with Stephanie:

Email: StephanieWagnerCT@gmail.com

Open Your Heart...Lend a Hand

Nothing is more satisfying than helping others, doing something kind or helpful and expecting nothing in return. You have no expectation of recognition or gratitude—just the personal satisfaction of knowing you did something that brought joy to another person or improved someone's situation, either physically or emotionally.

I have been volunteering since I was young and have seen firsthand the difference it makes in the lives of others. I started in elementary school by doing volunteer work with the American Junior Red Cross, putting together care packages for people who did not have the most basic necessities. In junior high, I volunteered weekly at a nursing home. I would sit with the residents in their rooms, writing letters for them or chatting with them. My visits were about giving these seniors individual, undivided attention to let them know that someone cared about them, and that I was truly interested in hearing their stories and life experiences. Through this experience, I learned that sharing with others is so good for the soul.

All through high school, I volunteered for the Easter Seals. I was paired with the same client all those years, and each week I brought a different craft or art project to do with her. Every project was a hands-on project, which served as a form of occupational therapy for her. But even more important than the therapeutic purpose was the personal interaction the weekly visit provided each of us. We became good friends, and the visits were something we both looked forward to. The projects I brought were always a surprise, which she loved, and they were activities that made her feel productive and creative. Plus, she was creating something of beauty with her own two hands despite her physical challenges. My positive attitude helped her develop a more positive attitude.

My volunteer work continued once I went to college. I helped out in the art department at the Cotting School one day a week. It was a pleasure to encourage these children to express themselves through their artwork. Helping children develop a positive self-image is key to their success, and I felt honored to play a role in that process.

Throughout college, I also volunteered at the Walter E. Fernald State School. This was a school for children and adults whose families could no longer manage their care at home. These were people whose communities had forgotten them, and it was my privilege to volunteer there. I also did a practicum and completed my special education student teaching at Fernald. It warmed my heart to bring joy to people whom society had forsaken. State facilities are always short-staffed and always looking for additional help, and I saw firsthand that volunteering can be critical in making a difference in someone's life.

Through these experiences, I have learned that when you live in a community, you must contribute to that community. You must make a concerted effort to help improve the world for your neighbors, family and friends. After graduating from college, I became a special education teacher, and when I had my own children, I became very involved in the school PTO. That involvement continued through my children's school years, from kindergarten through high school. I learned that if you see something that needs improvement, do not criticize or complain; you are never helpful if you are part of the problem, so be positive and part of the solution. I was also a Cub Scout leader for ten years and ran weekly meetings for both of my sons when they were in elementary school. The boys worked on badges, service projects, and outdoor experiences. I hosted monthly leader meetings and volunteered for a week every summer at scout camp. Volunteering for these two organizations made a positive impact on many children while also bringing me joy.

I have also helped for quite a few years to assemble holiday baskets for visiting nurse patients. When you stop by people's homes with a basket of goodies, it tells the patient and their families that someone understands what they are going through and that someone cares. Small gestures are huge when a person is dealing with health issues. Never underestimate the impact a kind word or positive gesture can have on someone.

Today I am involved with the local Lions Club, which is an international service organization. I oversee the collection of eyeglasses that people no longer use and have fourteen collection sites throughout my town. The glasses are refurbished and sent throughout the world and distributed for free to people who have no other means to obtain prescription glasses, a true life-changer for the underprivileged. Glasses that most people would discard are some people's only chance to see clearly, and this is yet another way I can help.

All in all, my time spent volunteering has shown me that when you open your heart, you open your world to the endless possibilities there are, on a daily basis, to make this a better world for all of us.

Do you have a talent you would like to share? Do you have a special interest? Look around your neighborhood and explore your community to see where there is a need that you can fill. Consider getting involved with a local program or group seeking volunteers. Look for people who share your desire to help, and look to work with others who have similar interests. If you find a group that shares your interests and values, offer to get involved. Ask where they need assistance. You, as one individual, can absolutely make a difference.

Perhaps offer to help out once a month or every other week. Or, if your schedule allows, volunteer on a weekly basis. Always promise less and deliver more. Only commit to a time frame that is realistic for you, your work schedule, and your personal family commitments. If you make a commitment, it must be realistic; do not overextend yourself. Volunteer time that you can maintain so that your involvement is something you look forward to and enjoy. You can share your joy, experience and knowledge with others, and if you enjoy what you do, it will reflect in all of your interactions with others. Never underestimate the impact you can make as an individual person who truly cares. Believe in yourself, and believe that you can help improve other people's lives. You can make a difference.

* * *

Bio for Mike:

Mike A. Williams is an experienced multifaceted senior technology executive of global Fortune 500 companies in the technology, finance, insurance, logistics, and health industry verticals. Mike has over thirty years of managerial and executive experience leading large-scale digital business enabling operations.

Mike is a passionate developer of talent, a community advocate and philanthropist who invests his time, treasures and talent to advance communities and help nonprofit founders and entrepreneurs launch.

He is also a two-time author and regularly serves as a speaker, panelist and workshop leader on topics covering leadership, technology and diversity.

Connect with Mike:

Email: mrmikeawilliams@outlook.com
LinkedIn: linkedin.com/in/mrmikeawilliams

Giving is Life

It is one thing to live life, but another to live a purpose-driven life. When I say purpose, I am talking about identifying a cause or reason to exists beyond a paycheck, a career or even just simply living altogether. No matter who you are or what you do for a living, part of your purpose in life must include a way to give back to individuals and organizations. The power of philanthropy allows you to do just that.

When most people think of philanthropy, they just think of giving money. Unfortunately, many of us who are not financially able to give money believe we are therefore unable to give. That is simply not true; everyone can give. Giving is not just about donating money. In fact, there are several ways to give. The primary ways to give are your time, your talents and your treasures (money).

"Remember that the happiest people are not those getting more, but those giving more." –H. Jackson Brown Jr.

What is Philanthropy?

When you openly support and promote a cause that will benefit others, that is a form of philanthropy. Yes, monetary contributions can help advance and support charitable endeavors, but philanthropy is not just about money. There are several ways for everyone to give and help individuals and organizations:

Time: Of all the ways to give, time is truly the most precious. When you give time to a cause, you are essentially deducting time away from your personal or professional goals, your family or even your business. Unlike money, there is no abundance of time. We all have the same number of hours in a day; how we choose to use those hours will demonstrate how we choose to live and what our priorities are. Lending your time to support worthy causes is priceless.

Talent: We all have a skill that we may overlook that many individuals and organizations may need. Whether you are a computer repair technician, accountant, attorney or even a janitor, just about everyone has a talent that can help others. Also note that when you lend your talents, you also are giving your time. When it comes to philanthropy, there certainly is not a shortage of talent that can help, but there is a shortage of those willing to use their talents to help. Do not be one of those not willing to help.

Treasures: Most philanthropic activity comes from volunteers who lend their time and talents to assist in advancing a cause. However, while donating time and talents is wonderful and worthy, the two alone often are not enough. Many individuals and organizations need more than just volunteers with time and talent, they also need money. When you are able to give financially, you should do so. Some people may need help to pay their rent or buy food, or they require help with other essential needs to get by. Many charitable organizations need money to support their operational expenses and the programs they have established to help the broader community of people in need. We all know money is not everything, but we also know that money can mean everything in the short-term for those in need. If you can, give like someone's life depended on it. Oftentimes, it does.

Why You Should Give

Close your eyes and imagine being stripped of everything you own today; everything you have worked for is just gone in an instant. Who would help you? How would you survive? Would anyone even care? Every day, there is an individual or an organization supporting a cause that must contemplate one or all of these questions. The truth is, at any point, any of us can be in a situation where we need help, whether financially or otherwise. You should give because if you happen to be in need, you will want someone to help you. You give because you can help an individual who has fallen on hard times believe in themselves again; you give because you can help an organization advance their mission and continue to serve and help others; but most importantly, you give because it is the right thing to do. Giving is life. Giving just makes you feel damn good about yourself and those you help.

"You give because it is not only the right thing to do, but the thing to do that makes some things right." –Mike A. Williams

Be the Silent Hero

Philanthropy and giving in general are not about promoting what you do for organizations or anything you have done for others; it is simply about helping advance and support a cause. Silent heroes are those who do not promote themselves because they helped; they simply help and promote the cause and mission of the people and organizations they are helping. They also encourage others to get involved. Giving is not about you; it is about those you seek to help. Silent heroes are humble, purpose-driven individuals. They support causes that align with their passion and values. We need the next generation of silent heroes who understand the power of philanthropy.

Philanthropy is Powerful

According to Giving USA and the National Center for Charitable Statistics, Americans give over $400 billion and donate up to 8 billion hours (economic value of $190-plus billion) of volunteer time every year to U.S. charities. These numbers prove that philanthropy is truly powerful. Nonetheless, as powerful as philanthropy is, and with all of the money and time invested, there are always more problems, more causes and definitely a need for others like yourself to do your part. After graduation, consider adding your superpowers to philanthropy.

Just remember, you can give:
 Your time;
 Your talents;
 Your treasures.

Or even all three if you can. Philanthropy is powerful because of the people who are passionate about certain causes and are caring enough to help. Ultimately, that sentence should describe all of us.

* * *

Activity: How to Give Back

Mike A. Williams highlighted how you can give in three different ways:

1. Your time
2. Your talents
3. Your treasures

For this activity, document how you have used your time, your talents and your treasures by answering the following questions:

How you have given in the past:

_____

_____

_____

_____

_____

_____

How you can give back today:

_____

_____

_____

_____

_____

_____

How you want to give back in the future:

_____

_____

_____

_____

_____

_____

_____

ACKNOWLEDGEMENTS

Thank you to my wife for her unwavering support of all of my different dreams, ideas and projects.

Thank you to the amazing people who contributed their stories to this book. Your willingness to share is what makes this impactful for those reading it.

Thank you Kate Kormushoff for the cover design and artistic flare you added to the book.

Thank you Meghan Hayden, owner of River Bend Bookshop, who helped get this book published.

Thank you to my amazing editor who helped get the book to the version you just completed.

When I first had the idea to write this book, I knew immediately I wanted it to be a collection of stories from a variety of people. Diversity of thought helps us grow as individuals and meaningfully contribute to our personal and professional lives. This book showcases the diverse experiences from people in a variety of industries.

Learn from the stories, the experiences, the good and the bad. Each of these individuals shared personal anecdotes that I hope you enjoyed. Feel free to connect with any of them to learn more about their journeys. Thank you for reading, and best of luck on your journey.

CPSIA information can be obtained
at www.ICGtesting.com
Printed in the USA
FSHW021817030521

9 781954 975002